"That from these honored dead
we take increased devotion
to that cause for which they gave
the last full measure of devotion."

**Abraham Lincoln
Address at Gettysburg
Nov. 19, 1863**

This book is dedicated to the men and women
of the United States armed forces who died
in Operations Desert Shield and Desert Storm.

DEDICATION

The Pentagon list of U.S. deaths during Operation Desert Shield and Operation Desert Storm. (Pentagon officials also report 357 wounded.)

Adams, Thomas R., Baton Rouge, La.
Alaniz, Andy, Corpus Christi, Texas
Allen, Frank C., Waianae, Hawaii
Allen, Michael R., West Point, Miss.
Ames, David R., Schuyler Lake, N.Y.
Anderson, Michael, Clarksville, Tenn.
Applegate, Tony R., Portsmouth, Ohio
Arteaga, Jorge I., Trumbull, Conn.
Atherton, Steven E., Nurmine, Pa.
Auger, Allen M., West Boylston, Mass.
Avey, Hans Christian Richard,
hometown unknown
Awalt, Russell F., hometown unknown
Bartusiak, Stanley W., Romulus, Mich.
Bates, Tommie, Coventry, R.I.
Beaudoin, Cindy M., Plainfield, Conn.
Belas, Lee A., Port Orchard, Wash.
Belliveau, Michael L., of Colorado;
hometown unknown
Bentzlin, Stephen E., Wood Lake, Minn.
Benz, Kurtz A., Garden City, Mich.
Betz, Dennis W., Alliance, Ohio
Bland, Thomas Clifford Jr.,
Gaithersburg, Md.
Blessinger, John P., Ft. Walton Beach, Fla.
Blue, Tommy A., Ft. Bliss, Texas
Bnosky, Jeffrey J., Schuylkill County, Pa.
Boliver, John A., Monongahela, Pa.
Bongiorni, Joseph P., Morgantown, W. Va.
Bowman, Charles L. Jr., Manchester, Md.
Boxler, John T., Johnstown, Pa.
Brace, William C., Fountain Hill, Pa.
Bradt, Douglas L., Houston
Bridges, Cindy D.J., Trinity, Ala.
Brilinski, Roger P. Jr., Ossineke, Mich.
Brooks, Tyrone M., Detroit
Brown, Christopher B., Leslie, Ga.
Brown, Darrell K., Memphis, Tenn.
Buege, Paul G., Mary Esther, Fla.
Burt, Paul L., Hingham, Mass.
Butler, Tommy D., Amarillo, Texas
Butts, William T., Waterford, Conn.
Cady, Andrew T., Florence, Ore.
Caldwell, Thomas R., Columbus, Ohio
Calloway, Kevin Lee, Arpin, Wis.
Campisi, John, Covina, Calif.
Carr, Jason C., Halifax, Va.
Carrington, Monray C., North
Braddock, Pa.
Cash, Clarence A., Ashland, Ohio
Chase, Richard W., San Antonio, Texas
Clark, Barry M., Hurlburt Field, Fla.
Clark, Beverly S., Armagh, Pa.
Clark, Larry M., Decatur, Ga.

Clark, Steven Douglas, Cedar Rapids, Iowa
Cleyman, Marc H., Jacksonville Beach, Fla.
Collins, Melford R., Uhland, Texas
Connelly, Mark A., Lancaster, Pa.
Cooper, Ardon B., Seattle
Cooper, Dallas, Russellville, Mo.
Costen, William T., St. Louis
Cotto, Ismael, New York
Craver, Alan B., Penn Hills, Pa.
Cronin, William D. Jr., Elmhurst, Ill.
Crumby, David R. Jr., Long Beach, Calif.
Dailey, Michael C. Jr, Klamath Falls, Ore.
Damian, Roy T. Jr., Toto, Guam
Daniels, Michael D., hometown unknown
Danielson, Donald, Ft. Bragg, N.C.
Daugherty, Robert L. Jr., Hollywood, Fla.
Davila, Manuel A., Gillette, Wyo.
Davis, Marty R., Salina, Kan.
Dees, Tatiana, Tehran, Iran
Delagneau, Rolando A., Gretna, La.
Delgado, Delwin, Jacksonville, Fla.
Delgado, Luis, Laredo, Texas
Diffenbaugh, Thomas M., Bakersfield, Calif.
Dillon, Gary S., Du Page County, Ill.
Dillon, Young, Aurora, Colo.
Dolvin, Kevin R., Canton, Ohio
Donaldson, Patrick A., Corrigan, Texas
Douthit, David Q., Tacoma, Wash.
Dwyer, Robert J., Worthington, Ohio
Edwards, Jonathan R., Terrace, Ohio
Eichenlaub, Paul R. II, Bentonville, Ark.
Fajardo, Mario, Flushing, N.Y.
Farnen, Steven P., Columbia, Mo.
Felix, Eliseo, Avondale, Ariz.
Fielder, Douglas L., Nashville, Tenn.
Fitz, Michael L., Horicon, Wis.
Fleming, Anthony J., Buffalo, N.Y.
Fontaine, Gilbert A., Spring Valley, N.Y.
Fowler, John C., Beaumont, Texas
Galvan, Arthur, Navarre, Fla.
Gardner, Samuel M. Jr., Idalou, Texas
Garrett, Mike Allen, Laurel, Miss.
Garvey, Phillip M., Pensacola, Fla.
Garza, Arthur O., Kingsville, Texas
Garza, Daniel, San Antonio, Texas
Gay, Pamela Y., Surrey, Va.
Gentry, Kenneth B., Ringgold, Va.
Gillespie, John H., Yeadon, Pa.
Gilliland, David A., Warrensburg, Mo.
Godfrey, Robert G., Phenix City, Ala.
Gologram, Mark J., Alliance, Ohio
Gordon, John M., Spring, Texas
Graybeal, Daniel E., Johnson City, Tenn.
Gregory, Troy L., Richmond, Va.
Grimm, William D., Hurlburt Field, Fla.
Haddad, Albert G. Jr., Denton, Texas
Hailey, Garland V., Wadesboro, N.C.
Hampton, Tracy, of Mississippi;
hometown unknown
Hancock, Joe Henry Jr., Nashville, Tenn.
Harris, Michael A. Jr., Pollocksville, N.C.
Harrison, Timothy R., Maxwell, Iowa

Hart, Adrian J., Albuquerque, N.M.
Hatcher, Raymond E. Jr., Monticello, Fla.
Haws, Jimmy Dewayne, Travers, Calif.
Hawthorne, James D., Stinnett, Texas
Hector, Wade E., Newport, N.H.
Hedeen, Eric D., Malaga, Wash.
Hein, Kerry P., Sound Beach, N.Y.
Henderson, Barry K., Tuscumbia, Ala.
Henry-Garay, Luis A., Brooklyn, N.Y.
Herr, David R. Jr., Ft. Worth, Texas
Herrera, Rosendo, San Antonio, Texas
Heyden, James, Tuscumbia, Ala.
Heyman, David L., Hazelwood, Mo.
Hill, Timothy, Detroit
Hills, Kevin J., Genoa, Ill.
Hoage, Adam T., Corona, Calif.
Hodges, Robert K., Hurlburt Field, Fla.
Hogan, Harry G., Birmingham, Ala.
Holland, Donnie R., Bastrop, La.
Hollen, Duane W. Jr., Bellwood, Pa.
Hook, Peter Samuel, Bishop, Calif.
Horwath, Raymond L. Jr., Waukegan, Ill.
Howard, Aaron W., Battle Creek, Mich.
Hughes, Robert, Vernon, Conn.
Hulec, Rande J., Cleveland
Hull, Daniel V., Dallas
Hurley, Patrick R., New Douglas, Ill.
Hurley, William J., Cook County, Ill.
Hutchison, Mark E., Elkins, W.Va.
Hutto, John W., Andalusia, Ala.
Huyghue, Wilton L., St. Thomas,
Virgin Islands
Jackson, Arthur, Brent, Ala.
Jackson, Kenneth Jerome, Concord, N.C.
Jackson, Timothy J., Anniston, Ala.
James, Jimmy W., of New Jersey;
hometown unknown
Jenkins, Thomas A., Mariposa, Calif.
Jock, Dale William, Malone, N.Y.
Joel, Daniel D., Glenbeulah, Wis.
Jones, Alexander, St. Louis
Jones, Daniel M., Wakefield, Mass.
Jones, Glen D., Grand Rapids, Minn.
Jones, Phillip J., Atlanta
Josiah, Troy, St. Thomas, Virgin Islands
Kamm, Jonathan H., Mason, Ohio
Kanuha, Damon V., San Diego
Keller, Kenneth T., Cook County, Ill.
Kelly, Shannon, Gulf Breeze, Fla.
Kemp, Nathaniel H., Greenwood, Fla.
Keough, Frank S., North Huntington, Pa.
Kidd, Anthony W., Lima, Ohio
Kilkus, John R., Norfolk County, Maine
King, Jerry L., Winston-Salem, N.C.
Kirk, Reuben G. III, Dunlow, W.Va.
Knutson, Lonty A., San Antonio, Texas
Koritz, Thomas F., Rochelle, Ill.
Kramer, David W., Palm Desert, Calif.
Kutz, Edwin B., Sunnymead, Calif.
Lake, Victor T. Jr., Jacksonville, N.C.
LaMoureaux, Dustin Craig, Bremerton, Wash.
Lane, Brian L., Bedford, Ind.

Lang, James M., Pomfret, Md.
Lee, Richard R., Independence, Mo.
Lewis, Ralph E., hometown unknown
Linderman, Michael E. Jr., Roseburg, Ore.
Lindsey, Scott J., Diamond Springs, Calif.
Love, James H., Arnold, Md.
Lumpkins, James H., New Richmond, Ohio
Lupatsky, Daniel, Centralia, Pa.
Madison, Anthony, Monessen, Pa.
Mahan, Gary, Waco, Texas
Maks, Joseph D., Roseburg, Ore.
Malak, George N., Santa Monica, Calif.
Manns, Michael N. Jr., Fredericksburg, Va.
Martin, Christopher, hometown unknown
Mason, Steven G., Paragould, Ark.
Matthews, Kelly L., Buckley, Mich.
May, James B. II, Ft. Walton Beach, Fla.
Mayes, Christine L., Rochester Mills, Pa.
McCarthy, Eugene, Brooklyn, N.Y.
McCoy, James R., Wilmington, Del.
McCreight, Brent A., Eminence, Ky.
McDougle, Melvin D., Fayetteville, N.C.
McKinney, Carol, Leslie, Mo.
McKinsey, Daniel C., Hanover, Pa.
Middleton, Jeffrey T., Oxford, Kan.
Miller, James R. Jr., Decatur, Ind.
Miller, Mark A., Cannelton, Ind.
Mills, Michael W., Jefferson, Iowa
Mitchell, Adrienne L., Moreno Valley, Calif.
Mobley, Phillip D., Blue Springs, Mo.
Moller, Nels A., Paul, Idaho
Mongrella, Garett A., Belvidere, N.J.
Monroe, Michael N., Auburn, Wash.
Monsen, Lance M., Pembine, Wis.
Montalvo, Candelario, Eagle Pass, Texas
Moran, Thomas J., Cornwallis Heights, Pa.
Morgan, Donald, Ford, Va.
Morgan, John K., Bellevue, Wash.
Murphy, Joe, Roosevelt, N.Y.
Murray, James C. Jr., Conroe, Texas
Neel, Randy L., Albuquerque, N.M.
Nelson, Rocky J., New Auburn, Wis.
Noline, Michael A., Phoenix, Ariz.
Noonan, Robert, Cincinnati
O'Brien, Cheryl L., Long Beach, Calif.
Oelschlager, John L., Niceville, Fla.
Oliver, Arthur D., Atlanta
Olson, Jeffry Jon, Grand Forks, N.D.
Olson, Patrick B., Washington, N.C.
Ortiz, Pat Bouvier E., Ridgewood, N.Y.
Pack, Aaron A., Phoenix, Ariz.
Palmer, William E., Hillsdale, Mich.
Parker, Fred R. Jr., Reidsville, N.C.
Patterson, Anthony T., Oxnard, Calif.
Paulson, Dale L., Sacramento, Calif.
Perez, Daniel G., San Antonio, Texas
Perry, Kenneth J., Lake Waccamaw, N.C.
Phillips, Kelly D., Madison Heights, Mich.
Plasch, David G., Portsmouth, N.H.
Plummer, Marvin J., Ponte Vedra
Beach, Fla.
Plunk, Terry, Vinton, Va.

Poole, Ramono L., Muscle Shoals, Ala.
Poremba, Kip A., Springfield, Va.
Porter, Christian J., Wood Dale, Ill.
Poulet, James Bernard, San Carlos, Calif.
Powell, Dodge R., Hollywood, Fla.
Price, Richard M., San Antonio, Texas
Randazzo, Ronald M., Glen Burnie, Md.
Reel, Jeffrey D., Vincennes, Ind.
Reichle, Hal H., Marietta, Ga.
Reid, Fredrick A., Harrisburg, Pa.
Rennison, Ronald D., Dubuque, Iowa
Ritch, Todd C., Charlestown, N.H.
Rivera, Manuel Jr., New York
Rivers, Ernest, Anderson, S.C.
Robson, Michael R., Seminole, Fla.
Rodriguez, Eloy A. Jr., Key West, Fla.
Rollins, Jeffrey A., Bountiful, Utah
Romel, Timothy W., Alameda, Calif.
Rose, Peter, Lincoln, Neb.
Rossi, Marie T., Oradell, N.J.
Rush, Scott A., Blaine, Minn.
Russ, Leonard A., Pleasantville, N.J.
Sanders, Henry J. Jr., Cocoa, Fla.
Sapien, Manuel B. Jr., Denver
Satchell, Baldwin, Cortland, Ala.
Schiedler, Mattew J., Hubbard, Ore.
Schmauss, Mark J., Hurlburt Field, Fla.
Schramm, Stephen G., Birmingham, Ala.
Schroeder, Scott A., Milwaukee
Schuldt, Bradley R., Arlington Heights, Ill.
Schwartzendruber, George R., San Diego
Scott, Brian P., Park Falls, Wis.
Seay, Timothy B., Thomaston, Ga.
Settimi, Jeffrey A., Ft. Wayne, Ind.
Shaw, Timothy A., Suitland, Md.
Sheffield, Edward E., San Antonio, Texas
Shukers, Jeffrey W., Union, Iowa
Siko, Stephen J., Latrobe, Pa.
Simpson, Brian K., Indianapolis
Smith, James A. Jr., Somerville, Tenn.
Smith, Michael S., Erie, Pa.
Smith, Russell G. Jr., Fall River, Mass.
Snyder, David T., Kenmore, N.Y.
Snyder, John M., Milltown, N.J.
Spackman, Brian K., Niles, Ohio
Speicher, Jeffrey W., Ft. Bragg, N.C.
Spellacy, David, Columbus, Ohio
Stephens, Christopher H., Houston
Stephens, John B., Morristown, Tenn.
Stephenson, Dion J., Bountiful, Utah
Stewart, Anthony D., Yonkers, N.Y.
Stewart, Roderick T., Shreveport, La.
Stokes, Adrian, Riverside, Calif.
Stone, Thomas G., Falconer, N.Y.
Streeter, Gary E., Manhattan, Kan.
Strehlow, William A., Kenosha, Wis.
Stribling, Earl K., Gilbert, La.
Swano, Peter L. Jr., Salem, N.Y.
Sylvia, James H., Putnam, Conn.
Talley, Robert D., Newark, N.J.
Tapley, David L., Winton, Calif.
Tatum, James D., Athens, Tenn.

Thomas, Phillip J., Chapel Hill, N.C.
Thorp, James K., Valley Station, Ky.
Tillar, Donaldson P. III, Miller School, Va.
Tormanen, Thomas R., Milford, Mich.
Trautman, Steven R., Houstonia, Miss.
Turner, Charles J., Richfield, Minn.
Underwood, Reginald C., Lexington, Ky.
Valentine, Roger E., Memphis, Tenn.
Velazquez, Mario Vega, Ponce, Puerto Rico
Vigrass, Scott N., Tonawanda, N.Y.
Villarreal, Carpio Jr., San Antonio, Texas
Viquez, Carlos A., Bronx, N.Y.
Volden, Robert L., New York
Wade, Robert C., Hackensack, N.J.
Waldron, James E., Jeannett, Pa.
Walker, Charles S., Jonesboro, Ga.
Walker, Daniel B., Whitehouse, Texas
Walls, Frank J., Hawthorne, Pa.
Walrath, Thomas E., Saratoga Springs, N.Y.
Walters, Dixon L. Jr., Navarre, Fla.
Wanke, Patrick A., Watertown, Wis.
Ware, Bobby M., New Burn, N.C.
Warne, David A., Fair Oaks, Calif.
Weaver, Brian P., Lockport, N.Y.
Weaver, Paul J., Navarre, Fla.
Wedgwood, Troy M., The Dalles, Ore.
Welch, Lawrence N., Chisholm, Minn.
Whittenburg, Scotty L., Carlisle, Ark.
Wieczorek, David M., Gentry, Ark.
Wilbourn, James N., Huntsville, Ala.
Wilcher, James, Crystal Springs, Miss.
Wilkinson, Philip L., Savannah, Ga.
Williams, Jonathan M., Portsmouth, Va.
Winkle, Corey L., Lubbock, Texas
Winkley, Bernard S., Windsor, Maine
Witzke, Harold P. III, Caroga Lake, N.Y.
Wolverton, Richard V., Latrobe, Pa.
Worthy, James E., Albany, Ga.
Wright, Kevin E., Louisville, Ky.
Zeugner, Thomas C.M., Petersburg, Va.

Missing in action:
Connor, Patrick K., Virginia Beach, Va.
Cooke, Barry T., Virginia Beach, Va.
Phillis, Stephen Richard, Rock Island, Ill.
Speicher, Michael Scott, Jacksonville,
Fla. (Pentagon officials believe this
downed pilot was dead, but listed him
as missing because his body had not
been recovered.)

CONTENTS

Page 5:

Josh McCrary, 4, hugs his father, Army Sgt. 1C John McCrary of the 475th Engineering Platoon, based in El Dorado, Kan., in November before he left for active duty. McCrary said, "I hate to leave my family, but I would rather fight ... over there, rather than having them over here."

JEFF TUTTLE
Wichita Eagle

Pages 6 and 7:

Nurse Amy Stuart of the 5th Mobile Army Surgical Hospital snuggles with a teddy bear she received from her family as she takes a nap on a cot in Saudi Arabia shortly before the ground war began.

DAVID C. TURNLEY
Detroit Free Press

This page:

James Evans of the Kentucky National Guard's 217th Quartefmaster Detachment watches the sun rise over the Persian Gulf on his third day in Saudi Arabia.

RON GARRISON
Lexington Herald-Leader

EYE
OF THE
STORM

Images of the Persian Gulf War
by Knight-Ridder photographers

Edited by Randy Miller
Written by Gary Blonston

Knight-Ridder, Inc.
Miami, Fla.

Published in 1991 by
Knight-Ridder, Inc.
One Herald Plaza
Miami, Fla. 33132

Library of Congress Catalog Card Number 91-090286

ISBN 0-937247-22-7

Produced by the Detroit Free Press
321 W. Lafayette Blvd.
Detroit, Mich. 48226

Distributed by Quality Mailing Service
3333 W. Fort St.
Detroit, Mich. 48216

Printed in the United States of America

10 9 8 7 6 5 4 3 2 1
First edition

A U.S. Humvee all-purpose
vehicle guards a column of Iraqi
troops that surrendered to
members of the 2nd Marine
Division on the second day of
the ground war. More than
63,000 Iraqis were taken
prisoner during the war.
TODD BUCHANAN
Philadelphia Inquirer

INTRODUCTION

A photographic book is perhaps the best way to reflect the scope of the Persian Gulf War's impact and to provide a perspective on its events. Photographs, it seems, have an advantage in documenting history. They can inform us without misrepresentation or ambiguity, as a detached observer of unfolding events, and at the same time resurrect memories that make us taste the experience once more.

The book you hold contains the work of 36 photographers from 20 newspapers across the country. These images are not just from the Persian Gulf, because the war also took place in our homes, on our televisions and in our streets. We debated it at work and considered it, as we lay in bed, in late-night conversations. We shouted our support in yellow ribbons adorned on trees and in our demonstrations, both pro and con, that clarified our emotions.

As we remember the events of the war, this work will remain as a national scrapbook of our experience. It is testament to both our divided sentiments and common memories of a very uncommon war.

Randy Miller

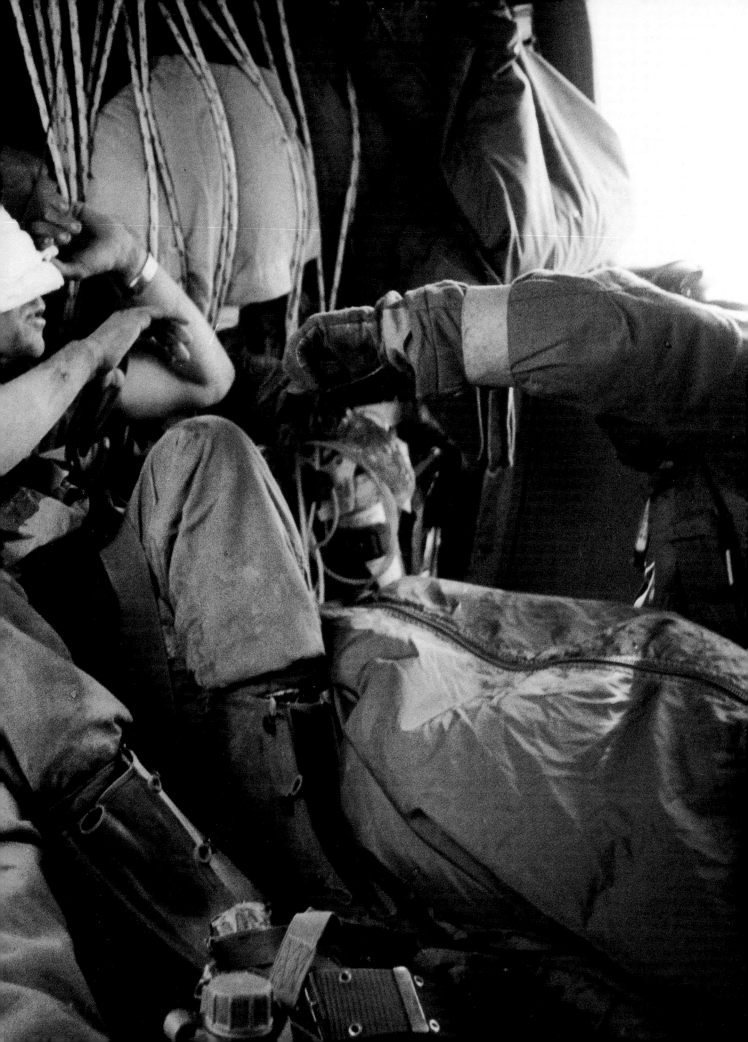

A MEASURE OF PRIDE

By Gary Blonston

In some ways, the Persian Gulf War of 1991 was typical of war as it has been fought over ageless time: An exercise in mass violence, waged in the name of security and peace. The least civil act of any civilized society, but the glue that bonds a nation like no other. The most ruinous arena humankind can choose, but in a perverse, adrenal way, the greatest show on Earth.

For the United States, for its president, its military and millions of edgy Americans, there was one thing different about this war. Whether the United States and more than two dozen other countries in the United Nations-supported coalition could prevail over Iraq was not really an issue. But unless American forces could lead the allies to win decisively and well, the United States would be a loser just the same, in the eyes of the world, in the eyes of its own people.

President George Bush called it a war for freedom from tyranny, Saddam Hussein's tyranny over Kuwait. Secretary of State James Baker III called it a war for a way of life dependent on a reliable, reasonably priced supply of oil. Beneath the rhetoric and the realpolitik, it offered something else as well: the opportunity to regain what the country had lost to Vietnam, to Khomeini's Iran, to Japan, to the savings and loan industry, to budgetary irresponsibility and domestic stall. It was a war for pride.

In August 1990, when the first troops shipped out for the gulf, no one knew America's true military capabilities, the nature of the costs it might face or the strength of its resolve. The only relevant measures were measures of failure dating back to Vietnam.

Seven months later, in February 1991, flags and yellow ribbons flew as America waited to welcome home a triumphant multitude of men and women in desert camouflage, mourning but a few and flashing the venerable V sign inherited from the old, last war it won.

Capt. Mike Brown of the Union City, Calif., Fire Department was upset when city officials ordered fire fighters to remove flags from their trucks and helmets, so he opted for a new hairstyle in February.
MICHAEL RONDOU
San Jose Mercury News

Jeff Shaw says good-bye to wife, Pam, before leaving Ft. Jackson, S.C., for Operation Desert Storm on Nov. 5. Shaw is a member of the 132nd Military Police National Guard unit.

JAMIE FRANCIS
The State, Columbia, S.C.

Not for nearly a half-century, since World War II, had the United States experienced such a consoling wash of feelings: Relief and amazement, satisfaction and pride. A major national commitment had gone well for a change.

Vietnam War historian James Olson summed it up: "We've had this sense that we're the good guys, that we can make a difference in a fight for right. We did it in World War I, we did it in World War II, and then we screwed up in Vietnam. Now we're back."

That military success seemed a sign that the nation had unexploited capabilities for other work as well – peacetime progress, world leadership – based on the simple fact that the country had done what it set out to do. Along the way, it had gained a new set of heroes after a long time without any: Schwarzkopf, Powell, Bush and the half-million over there who did the work. It had achieved a moral triumph over an enemy who made himself so personally repellent that many Americans, many American soldiers and the president himself felt the war truly was against one man – Saddam Hussein. It had re-established its waning global reputation with a single geopolitical stroke. It had put on a fearsome and instructive display of devastation, starkly defining the difference between the First World and the Third.

In the weeks after Operation Desert Storm ended, the pain of personal loss and the horror of what had happened to civilian life in Iraq intruded on the national victory dance; the potential for more trouble in the gulf made the winning less conclusive, and the emerging details of the campaign inevitably revealed cracks and flaws.

But for all that, the country had acquired new benchmarks for influence in the world and confident commitment at home. After all the years of mixed feelings, millions discovered that it suddenly had become easy to feel . . . American.

Early in March, after the war was won, Nancy Shaw, 44, of Greenbelt, Md., felt that change powerfully as she stood in a chilly wind at Andrews Air Force Base, waiting with her young nephew to honor 21 strangers from other towns – the returning American prisoners of the Persian Gulf War. As she waited, she said something that seemed to apply to thousands of others in the crowd around her and to countless more across the country: "I never felt so proud. I've never wanted to be part of something so bad."

The dark recollections of Vietnam, the denunciations of George Bush as a warmonger, the discomforting awareness that one of the most advanced nations on the planet could find no solution to this regional episode short of going to war – nearly all those thoughts were gone, as if they indeed had been swept by a desert storm.

In the grand tapestry of military history, this was not a war likely to occupy a very large spot. In the story of the late 20th Century, it likely would not even rank with the reforms that had come to Eastern Europe, without war, in the years just before. Still, to most Americans with relatives, friends and loved ones at risk in the Persian Gulf, the outcome was miraculous, a precious gift they accepted with grateful, homecoming tears. For them, it was the most important war ever.

The same war that stirred such visceral pride in some, though, stirred

Anthony Romero of Arvada, Colo., displays his flag as he works in March on a house in Lousiville, near Denver.
CLIFF GRASSMICK
Boulder Daily Camera

July 17: *Iraqi President Saddam Hussein, his economy wounded by the 1980-88 Iran-Iraq war, threatens to use force against Kuwait if it does not curb oil production. Although Kuwait lent Hussein $15 billion during the war with Iran, he believes overproduction has lowered prices and cost his country billions.*

July 21-22: *Hussein begins moving 30,000 troops and tanks and rockets to Iraq's border with Kuwait.*

Aug. 1: *Iraqi officials walk out of talks in Saudi Arabia, complaining that Kuwaiti representatives were not negotiating seriously. Up to 100,000 Iraqi troops are massed at the border.*

Aug. 2: *Iraqi troops and tanks storm into Kuwait at dawn and move into the capital, Kuwait City, hours later. The emir of Kuwait, Sheikh Jaber al-Ahmed al-Sabah, flees. Hussein announces that the government of Kuwait has been overthrown. The United States denounces the invasion and freezes Iraqi assets. Gasoline prices increase.*

revulsion and disgust in others. They were the ones who had been stunned and angered by the idea of war even before they saw its cold technology and its human toll. To them, the masses who cheered the outcome seemed thoughtless and blithely jingoistic, and the homecoming celebrations seemed a carnival diversion from the true point as they saw it – that the United States was wrong to intervene, fight, destroy and kill in the first place. But the relative few who opposed the war were not much heard in the course of the conflict. The huge and supportive majority drowned them out, almost oblivious to their cries.

The very softest, fewest voices belonged to those who had felt the war most directly, not as a subject for debate or protest but as a private stab in the heart. For the Americans who cherished the 333 troops lost during the seven-month operation – only about 40 percent of them killed in combat – the Persian Gulf conflict was war as war has always been: random, unforgiving, an irresolvable collision between love and duty, patriotism and pain. They knew the warriors. They knew the war.

In a dramatically different way, so did thousands of Kuwaitis, murdered,

kidnapped, abused and plundered by the Iraqi invasion force. As they continue the daunting process of reconstruction, it is clear their memory of the war will last for many years more.

Those who knew wartime at its fullest, of course, were the dead, wounded and dispirited of Iraq. They had felt its cost for eight years even before allied planes suddenly appeared in the early morning skies, and when the six-week campaign against them was done, they felt it still, fighting on among themselves as if they couldn't stop.

From their side, the war was what United Nations authorities later called "near-apocalyptic," a recurring nightmare of air power that tore at Iraq's cities, devastated its military and created a strafed, bombed-out graveyard of people and vehicles on the broad highway from Kuwait City to Iraq, the failed escape route of an army in panicked retreat.

Seven months earlier, that ruined army of battered military vehicles, commandeered trucks and stolen cars had been an invasion force of tanks, troop carriers and artillery rolling the other way down that road, advancing as boldly and brashly as the man who ordered the assault.

Aug. 6: *United Nations imposes worldwide trade embargo.*

Aug. 7: *President George Bush announces he has ordered thousands of troops to Saudi Arabia to join a multinational force to deter Iraqi aggression; some troops had already arrived.*

Aug. 9: *Hussein announces that foreigners may not leave Iraq.*

Aug. 10: *The Arab League votes to send forces to Saudi Arabia.*

Aug. 17: *Bush calls up thousands of reservists. Iraq moves hostages to military sites.*

Aug. 25: *UN approves use of force to enforce embargo.*

Aug. 28: *Iraq starts releasing women and children hostages.*

Sept. 9: *Bush and Soviet President Mikhail Gorbachev meet in Helsinki, Finland, and show solidarity against Hussein.*

In response came the American-led allies, to mass on the other side of
George Bush's "line in the sand" and contend just as boldly that Hussein must
abandon his adventure in power politics and oil prices and take his forces
home.

From the moment Bush drew that line, both those in allied desert garb
and those in Iraqi drab knew that, whatever politicians said, whatever
tacticians hoped and loved ones prayed, the looming war would be expensive,
ferocious, more sophisticated and therefore more dangerous than any war in
modern times. For the first five months, neither side knew which one might
suffer more.

Waiting: Strangers in a strange land

Given choices, almost no one chooses to sit in the desert of Saudi Arabia in August. Its heat squeezes minds and crumples knees. It is featureless, empty to the horizon, dusty, glaring, wearing.

For American soldiers newly landed in the birthplace of Islam, there was little that resembled home, church, community or even the military bases from which most had come. Many had trained in the deserts of southern California, Texas and other parts of the American Southwest, but in such a culturally remote and rigid society as Saudi Arabia's, they felt they were doing more than their share of adapting, hiding their religions, hiding their flags, buttoning sleeves over female forearms and sticking close to quarters, so not to offend the people they had come to protect.

Most of the American forces were neither seasoned warriors nor worldly sophisticates. They were, by and large, young men and women who had taken a chance on the peacetime military as the best available job, whose experience overseas, if any, was likely to have been West Germany or an occasional stop in a foreign port. For the reservists among them, the jolt was even greater. Most never imagined their civilian soldiering would take them to a foreign war.

Long before there was war, for nearly every soldier in the field, simply being in Saudi Arabia was an ongoing assault. Spiritually and physically parching, it was a beer-ad of a place without the beer, distant in ways that couldn't be measured in mere miles and time zones.

The first troops arrived Aug. 7, and many of them thought, wishfully, that they would be home by Thanksgiving. They hated the waiting, but they could wait. They were professionals. Still, there was a big opposing army assembled

Edward Bazner, father of ex-hostage Kevin Bazner, welcomes his son, left, and daughter-in-law Dawn near Houston on Dec. 9 after Kevin arrived on a flight from Baghdad. The Bazners, of Palm Desert, Calif., were trapped during the invasion as they changed planes in Kuwait; his wife and children were allowed to leave in September.
PATRICIA BECK
Detroit Free Press

Sept. 25: *UN votes to cut off air traffic to and from Iraq.*

Oct. 15: *Defense Secretary Dick Cheney says U.S. troops will stay in the gulf indefinitely, for years if necessary, but asserts that sanctions are working.*

Oct. 31: *Bush declares: "I've had it" with Iraq's treatment of U.S. hostages.*

Nov. 8: *Bush announces plans to double U.S. forces in the gulf to more than 400,000.*

Nov. 19: *Iraq sends 250,000 more troops to Kuwait. Its total force in southern Iraq and Kuwait will approach 545,000.*

Nov. 29: *UN authorizes using force against Iraq and sets Jan. 15 withdrawal deadline.*

just across the border, and after a while the distant fact of it began to scratch like some desert bug. "Let's rock and roll," the fighter pilots said.

There was less enthusiasm for rocking and rolling at home. As supportive as most Americans were of Bush's tough stance, fewer relished a war of such ambiguous purpose and fearsome possibilities. The United Nations and much of the Democratic Congress didn't want a war as long as an economic embargo might drive Saddam Hussein's armies home. And so, while Americans still were learning how to say Saddam (Bush, for one, studiously avoided ever learning), they also were considering such phrases as "let the sanctions work," "no blood for oil" and "no more Vietnams," a thought that cut both ways in the debate about whether to go to war and how much to commit.

Antiwar activists, pacifists, isolationists, causists of every issue from gay rights to District of Columbia statehood came out to chant, march and protest, seasoned by the Vietnam era or taught by those who were.

But after the first rush of activism, most of the protests were small. The mass of the American people had not had time to hate the war in the Middle East the way they had come to abhor the war in southeast Asia.

There was an unanswered question in those early months, though: What was the country's staying power? Commentators warned ominously that the nation was soft, gun-shy, had no tolerance for American losses and no interest in fighting to protect the oil supplies of Western Europe and Japan.

Saddam Hussein, for one, seemed to believe that, and he worked the subject repeatedly in his florid radio and television broadcasts. Perhaps in

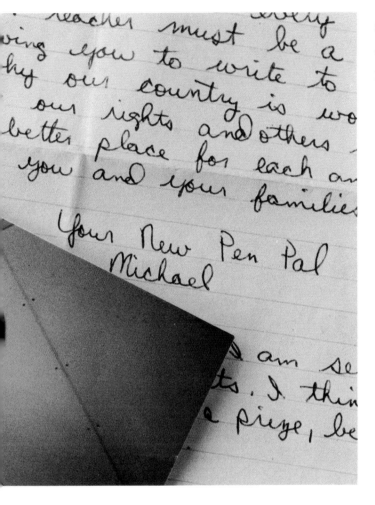

"I asked for his picture, and he sent it," 9-year-old Dearborn Heights, Mich., student Nicole Martinez said proudly of her letter from Army E4 Spec. Michael Buell of Southfield, Mich. She and her fourth-grade classmates wrote to "any soldier" in Saudi Arabia as a class project.

PATRICIA BECK
Detroit Free Press

some degree, the Bush administration believed it, too. The administration's military policy had a central goal of minimizing U.S. casualties, and that proved to be effective political insurance that those skeptical theories never would be tested. Until the final four days of ground fighting, the war seemed antiseptic and palatable when viewed from afar. Even when the fighting hit the desert floor, American losses were incredibly low. The country could live with that.

Dec. 6: *Hussein begins to release remaining hostages.*

Dec. 8: *U.S. begins to evacuate embassy in Kuwait.*

Jan. 9: *Geneva talks between Secretary of State James Baker and Iraqi Foreign Minister Tariq Aziz fail to break impasse.*

Jan. 12: *Congress authorizes use of force. Last U.S. diplomats leave Baghdad.*

Jan. 13: *UN chief Javier Perez de Cuellar meets Hussein, declares session fruitless.*

Jan. 15: *On deadline day, UN chief makes plea for peace.*

But no one could be sure of such outcomes as the autumn of 1990 arrived, and there seemed so much to fear:

Hussein's troops might move on Saudi Arabia before enough allied forces were in place to stop them.

Iraq might complete a nuclear weapon, or use chemicals, or germ warfare.

Western hostages might be used as human shields.

American forces might be stalemated in the desert as they had been in the jungles two decades before.

The weapons might not work, the price of oil might go sky-high, American casualties might be huge, the country might reinstitute the draft, the allied coalition might break down, the Arab world might rise in anger.

Bush used stern, determined words throughout those waiting days, but there were weeks when the word skittish seemed the best description of American opinion, not just at home but among the soldiers in the gulf as well. They were vulnerable to a close-by, numerically superior enemy, and they were reminded of that with every step as their gas masks, their constant companions, bumped a grim rhythm against their hips ... gas, gas, gas.

In November, things changed. The 200,000-troop complement in the gulf began to build toward more than 400,000, a defensive force becoming an

offensive force as the Bush administration readied for war. By the hundreds of thousands, more parents, wives and children felt their sons, husbands and fathers step sadly but resolutely from their grasp. And in this war as never before, daughters, wives and mothers shipped out, too, doing what they had to do, often with a special, unfamiliar sense of conflicted duty and heart-tearing loss that the whole country seemed to sense and share. Into a land that oppressed and denigrated women, they marched to do what their country no longer considered only a man's job.

By now, the desert had turned cooler, cool enough for battle. Allied troops drilled harder, tested weapons, moved around, stirring the sand and their own blood. Something was coming, and just in time.

Those soldiers had been aware, as they wondered how much support they were getting at home, that Americans were wondering about the military's staying power, too. The early months of discomfort in the desert *had* been wearing, the passing of Thanksgiving as hard as such times always are for soldiers in the field. As the months passed, some men who had left home as husbands had become fathers. Women who had said good-bye to their children had become deeply missed and missing. Vacant chairs sat forlornly at dining

The U.S. commander, Gen. H. Norman Schwarzkopf, shakes some desert sand out of his size 11 boots. Like many of his troops, he had ditched the standard Army-issue green-and-black jungle boots that let sand in.

DAVID C. TURNLEY
Detroit Free Press

room tables. There was a silent void at bedtime. Empty arms ached in the desert.

In the states, life had gone on. People had died. Money problems had arisen. Children's lives had been thrown in turmoil. Marriages had broken. The lines of distraught troops outside the judge-advocate's tents became longer, as more and more reasons came up to seek legal guidance over trouble back home.

Then, on Nov. 29, the UN Security Council passed the last of 12 resolutions it delivered against Iraq in the months after the occupation of Kuwait. Resolution 678 gave Iraq "one final opportunity" to pull out. Should it not be under way by Jan. 15, the United Nations would authorize the allied nations, by now 28 of them, to use "all means necessary" to restore Kuwait's freedom. Finally, the assembled mass of military men and women had something firm to look toward. They were ready, and they said so a thousand times a day. "We came to do a job," they said.

American officials said it didn't necessarily follow that a war would begin immediately after the deadline passed. They were right. It took 19 hours.

The air war: 39 days over Baghdad

On Jan. 16, just after 7 p.m. Washington time, presidential spokesman Marlin Fitzwater announced, "The liberation of Kuwait has begun."

So had the greatest application of battle technology the world had ever seen, and the most remarkable run of live television in history. What began

A Navy F14 fighter-bomber takes off from the USS John F. Kennedy in the Red Sea.

TODD BUCHANAN
Philadelphia Inquirer

with stunning, night-time views of Baghdad lit by anti-aircraft fire and exploding bombs became a daily display of the machinery of devastation:

Scud and Patriot missiles colliding in the dark sky, videotapes of laser-guided bombs plunging down air vents and through the doors of buildings, TV-guided missiles sending back a bomb's-eye view of targets that loomed larger and larger in the frame until the moment of destruction. The video-game designers had been right. That was how it would look.

But not always. Although "precision bombing" restricted to "military targets" never truly had been possible, that was what the military talked about, and in the early, innocent days of the war, that was what the country presumed from the videos the military showed. During the war, Iraq claimed that bombs had hit such civilian targets as a baby formula factory and a bomb shelter, but the Pentagon disputed those contentions. Whatever the truth of the specifics, it turned out that only 7 percent of the 88,500 tons of bombs dropped during the war were "smart," guided bombs. Damage assessment figures indicated that, of the unguided bombs, seven out of 10 had not hit their designated targets. "Surgical strike" had proven once more to be an oxymoron. UN observers looking at the devastation afterward reported that Iraq had been bombed back to "a pre-industrial age."

Accurate or not, the attacks were conclusive. Allied planes flew more than 116,000 sorties during the fighting, and only 75 aircraft were lost, just 42 of them to enemy fire. Saddam Hussein's Iraq became like the foolish knight in the Monty Python movie, dueling ineffectually as a superior opponent chopped off one limb, asked him to surrender, chopped off another, asked him again, chopped off another, and so forth. By the end – in fact well before the end – Iraq too had become limbless and lost.

The allied jets screamed and roared and bombed and fired for more than

Pilots climb into F14 Tomcats aboard the Kennedy during the first week of the air war.
TODD BUCHANAN
Philadelphia Inquirer

Jan. 16: *At 3 a.m. (7 p.m. EST), U.S., British, Saudi and Kuwaiti planes bomb Baghdad and other targets in Iraq and Kuwait on a moonless night. U.S. ships in the Persian Gulf launch over 100 cruise missiles. "The liberation of Kuwait has begun," Bush says.*

Jan. 17: *Iraq hits Israel with Scud missiles, a move that threatens to widen the war. The United States moves in Patriot missile batteries to knock down the Scuds.*

Jan. 21: *Iraq shows seven POWs, including three Americans, on television. "I am angry" about Iraq's vow to use the POWs as human shields against attack, Bush says.*

Jan. 25: *A massive oil spill spreads out into the Persian Gulf.*

Jan. 27: *Iraqi jets start flying to Iran, possibly to seek safety until after war ends. Smart bombs dropped on pumping equipment stanch the oil spill.*

Jan. 30: *The first major ground battle begins when Iraqi soldiers move into the abandoned Saudi border town of Khafji. More than 36 hours later, the allies claim victory, with 30 Iraqis killed, 400 taken prisoner.*

five weeks, until the commanders felt they could conduct the final phase of the war with the least possible resistance. This was the long-feared ground war, the unpredictable, telling time in this or any war when opposing armies come near enough to see each other's eyes.

The ground war: The last 100 hours

Saddam Hussein's soldiers didn't just blink. Some literally wept.

The ground war that had threatened to scatter American bodies over the

desert turned out to be hardly a war at all. Iraqi soldiers used no chemical weapons, Hussein unveiled no last-minute surprises, Iraqi artillery launched no lethal counterattack, and the supposedly formidable Republican Guard was quickly cornered and neutralized.

It was over in 100 hours, and thousands of front-line allied troops who had waited months for this moment in the sand saw no action at all. For them, the war had simply been a long, worrisome wait and a ride into the desert.

Iraqi troops surrendered by the tens of thousands, pleading for capture, kissing the hands of their keepers, turning themselves in to anyone they could find, even passing journalists. They appeared to feel little sense of guilt, failure or disloyalty. It seemed more that they had been the ones betrayed, long ago, when Hussein sent them, under-equipped and under-powered, to make their fruitless stand.

Some of the American soldiers who took charge of them clearly were embarrassed and awkward about the whole situation.

So incredible was the conclusion of the fighting that it raised a question for some analysts at home and some diplomats abroad that Americans could hardly have imagined a few months before: Had the war been won too well?

A member of the 2nd Marine
Division stands guard outside
Kuwait City shortly before Saudi
and Kuwaiti troops moved in to
retake the capital.
TODD BUCHANAN
Philadelphia Inquirer

Had it left the United States too comfortable with the idea of foreign intervention as a ready tool of national policy? Had it ruined Iraq too thoroughly, creating a Middle East power vacuum that might be filled by someone no less bellicose than Hussein? After years of criticism about wasteful spending and equipment that didn't work, had the American military been vindicated too completely, leaving the Congress and the country less able to say no in the future to such an assemblage of Pentagon heroes?

In the first months after the war, perhaps even in the first years, those questions were not likely to be answered. In the meantime, the homecoming parties, the loving personal reunions and the mass celebrations would continue, punctuated by Memorial Day and Fourth of July celebrations whose elaborate plans were under way even before the war was over. The funerals of those fallen in the gulf would continue for a while, too, private for the most part, less troubled by the glare of press and public attention that had accompanied the first few.

The last of the Desert Storm forces to die lost their lives after the war had ended, victims of happenstance, traffic accidents, crashes of aircraft on routine flights – deaths that happen to soldiers wherever they are posted, whatever their jobs.

Peace was setting in. Some of the troops would be in the gulf indefinitely, but most would return home. The country would get back to normal, welcome spring, pay its taxes, follow baseball, think less about the recovery of Kuwait and the fate of Iraq. It would hope there would be no more fighting, knowing that, militarily at least, the United States carried a bigger, more deterrent stick

Feb. 9: *Cheney and Gen. Colin Powell, chairman of the Joint Chiefs of Staff, visit top commanders in Saudi Arabia in what is seen as a prelude to a decision on a land war.*

Feb. 13: *The world sees pictures of charred bodies as Iraq claims an allied bomb hit a civilian shelter, killing hundreds. The allies insist the bunker was a military target.*

Feb. 15: *Iraq offers to leave Kuwait if Israel leaves the occupied territories and other conditions are met, but Bush rejects it as "a cruel hoax."*

Feb. 19: *Bush rejects a Soviet peace initiative, saying it "falls well short" of what is needed.*

Feb. 22: *Bush gives Iraq an ultimatum: Begin a "large-scale withdrawal" by noon the following day or face a bloody ground war.*

Feb. 23: *The deadline passes. That evening, a massive allied invasion begins. Bush declares, "The liberation of Kuwait has now entered a final phase."*

Feb. 24: *The U.S. commander in the gulf, Gen. H. Norman Schwarzkopf, says the allies achieved their first-day objectives within 10 hours and met only light resistance.*

than before, wielded by a president with unprecedented public approval.

A month after the tentative cease-fire in the gulf, when federal officials, celebrities and journalists gathered to joke with one another at Washington's annual Gridiron Dinner, Secretary of State Baker noted that the president, sitting near him at the speaker's table, seemed to be contemplating his glass of water. Baker wondered to the audience: Was Bush thinking of drinking it, parting it, or walking on it?

This was the same president whose ineffectual domestic performance had been a national joke the summer before. Things had changed that much.

Other things had changed: The whole world wanted to own weapons that could fly down air shafts. Some Arab nations seemed less hostile toward Israel, which had stayed out of the war despite the provocation of repeated missile attacks from Iraq. There was a run on war movies at the video stores. Gen. H. Norman Schwarzkopf rose from obscurity to international adulation, the wise, fair, hard-headed, soft-hearted, impossibly perfect symbol of what the American military always was supposed to be.

Eventually, though, the war fervor would ease, reality would set in, and some people would begin to say, fine, but does this have anything to do with budget deficits, education, environment, drugs, crime, poverty, civil rights, economic competitiveness, urban decay, infant mortality, AIDS, space stations, health care costs, the state of the financial industry, the airline industry, the auto industry?

The answer was, probably not. The war probably had been exactly what it seemed – a drama in three acts, waiting, warring and winning, then a curtain

call and a return to domestic life changed little now or in the future by the accomplishments of Desert Shield and Desert Storm.

The war had proven some things possible, some military achievements, some logistical feats, some political aims narrowly drawn and narrowly directed at a foreign provocateur who made it all easier by his recklessness and self-delusion.

But there is a difference between the hard-edged, irresistible demands of war and the compromised options of peacetime policy. Declaring war on domestic problems has been the redundant rhetoric of presidents in the last three decades. None ever has gone on to declare a victory.

The impact of this war on the people of the United States likely will have most to do with the point the country needed to prove when it entered the war in the first place: influence, standing, self-respect. The point was pride. Whatever else happened in the Persian Gulf and in the minds of Americans, the country won that point.

Gary Blonston in a national correspondent in the Washington bureau of Knight-Ridder Newspapers.

Feb. 25: *U.S. military officials report more than 20,000 Iraqis have been captured and allied troops are at the edge of Kuwait City. An Iraqi Scud missile lands on a military barracks near Dhahran, Saudi Arabia, killing 28 troops.*

Feb. 27: *After 100 hours of ground fighting, a cease-fire takes effect. "Kuwait is liberated. The Iraq army is defeated. Our military objectives are met," Bush says. Schwarzkopf discloses the U.S. strategy in the war, including pinning down Iraqi troops to wait for an amphibious attack in Kuwait that never came.*

March 3: *Iraqi commanders agree to peace terms and free 10 allied prisoners. Battles rage between rebel forces and government troops inside Iraq.*

March 5: *Iraq frees what it says are the last 35 allied prisoners.*

March 6: *Addressing Congress, Bush calls on Israelis and Arabs to end their conflict. He announces that the first planeload of U.S. troops is returning to the United States.*

IN THE BEGINNING

"Right now the biggest problem we have is that we're not able to tell our troops when we're going home. We've been told we need to prepare ourselves for at least a six-month stay. So we are planning our training and other activities through February 1991. If we get to come home earlier, all the better."

Maj. John E. Walus, Mt. Clemens, Mich.

America began to go to war on Aug. 6, 1990, when President George Bush sent the first contingent of U.S. troops to watch over the threatened border of Saudi Arabia. At first, though, the possibility of major conflict seemed remote. At the level of world politics, Iraq's invasion of Kuwait was troubling but not yet the stuff of regional war, and in the homes of service families, distance and separation wrung hearts more than the threat of combat.

For one thing, allied forces weren't numerous enough to confront Iraq for several months, and the United Nations' economic squeeze on Saddam Hussein sustained a hope that fighting might never be necessary. Three of the wealthiest oil nations on Earth and the largest armed coalition since World War II surely could find a way back to normal; the thought of what a war could do to oil fields, to wealth and to people seemed its own best deterrent.

But it wasn't. Even as antiwar protesters from San Francisco to Amman shouted their feelings, even as bored soldiers passed time and families prayed, Hussein refused to back off, the United Nations and the allies became more forceful, and war passed from distant possibility to clear and present danger.

Army Spec. 4 Hollie Vallance embraces her 7-week-old daughter, Cheyenne Vallance-Kirk, while her husband, Anthony Kirk, watches at Ft. Benning, Ga., in August. Vallance, of Galien, Mich., a 21-year-old medic with the 197th Infantry Brigade, hugged her child for 10 minutes before shipping out. In all, an estimated 27,000 women served in the Persian Gulf.

ALLEN HORNE
Columbus Ledger-Enquirer

Tom Barnhart of Simi Valley, Calif., salutes the USS Missouri as it leaves the Long Beach Naval Shipyard in November. His brother sailed with the frigate USS Ford, which escorted the Missouri to the Persian Gulf. In February, the Missouri fired its 16-inch guns in battle for the first time since the Korean War, pounding Iraqi positions in Kuwait prior to the ground war.

HAL WELLS
Long Beach Press-Telegram

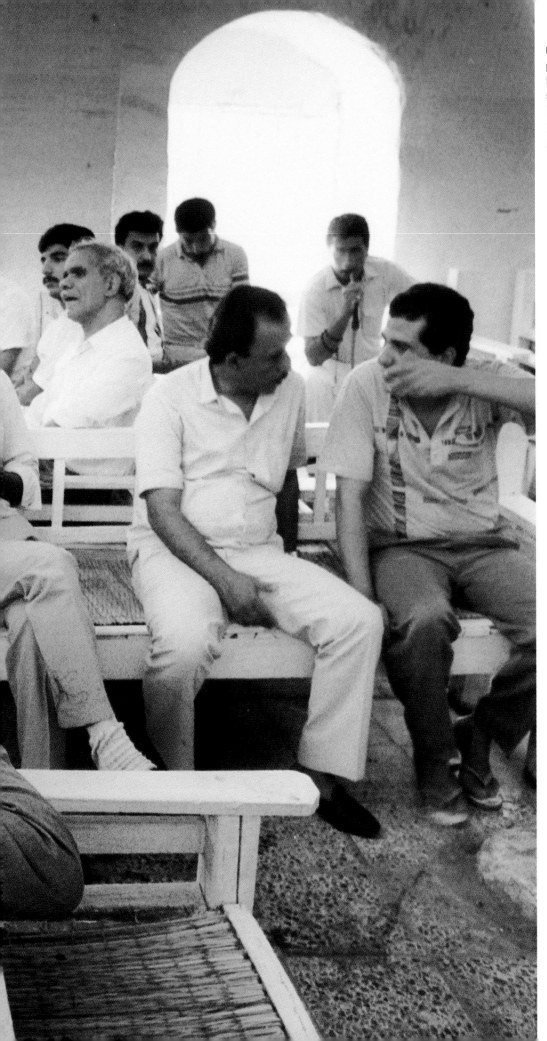

Underneath the ever-present photo of President Saddam Hussein, Iraqi men smoke and sip coffee in a Baghdad shop before the war.
DAVID C. TURNLEY
Detroit Free Press

Left:

Mavis Patterson, 74, attends a support-the-trooops rally in Homestead, Fla., her hometown. About 10,000 people at the rally formed the outline of the United States; a photo was put on postcards to send to troops in the Persian Gulf.

TOM ERVIN
Boca Raton News

Below:

Marianne Sutto, manager of the Mark Gregory Bridal Couture in Boca Raton, Fla., models a $15,000 silk and satin wedding dress designed by John Bradley. Bradley sold one of the dresses.

TOM ERVIN
Boca Raton News

Below, left:

Carol Baumgartner ties a yellow ribbon around a tree in Palo Alto, Calif. She spent $500 to buy 1,200 yards of ribbon to tie around trees near her office in Palo Alto.

PAUL KITAGAKI JR.
San Jose Mercury News

Below, right:

Members of the Marine Reserves' 4th Amphibious Assault Battalion bid farewell to loved ones at their Tampa, Fla., headquarters in November before heading to Camp Lejenue, N.C., after being activated for duty in Operation Desert Shield.

GRANT JEFFRIES
Bradenton Herald

Below:

Doctors, nurses, medical technicians and administrative workers from Keesler Air Force Base ship out in January from the Gulfport Air National Guard Center in Mississippi.

HERB WELCH
Biloxi Sun Herald

Right:

Army Pfc. Dawn Dorsch, 19, of Owendale, Mich., prepares a package to send to her fiance at the front in January. Dorsch was at an intermediary camp with a support battalion for the Army's 101st Airborne Division.

DAVID C. TURNLEY
Detroit Free Press

Left:

Lauri Pirkle bids farewell to her husband after giving him a dozen roses during a parade in Macon, Ga., in December. He was a member of the Georgia National Guard's 48th Infantry Brigade that was headed to California for desert training.

JAMES BORCHUCK
Macon Telegraph

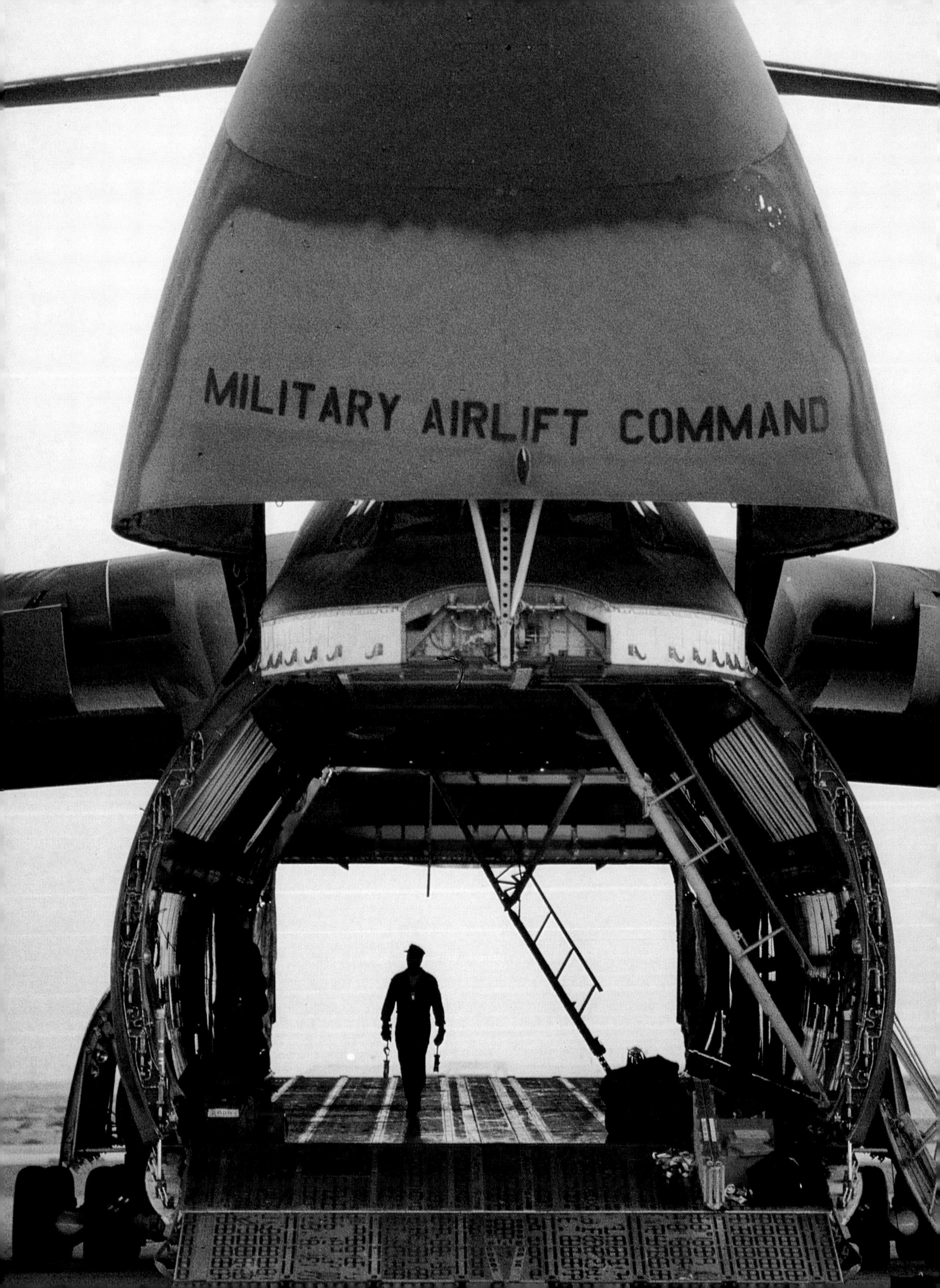
MILITARY AIRLIFT COMMAND

Left:

A soldier finishes unloading a U.S. C130 transport plane that brought soldiers and equipment from Germany. Tens of thousands of tons of material poured into Saudi Arabia in the months before the war.

JAMIE FRANCIS
The State, Columbia, S.C.

Below:

Members of the Kentucky National Guard's 217th Quartermaster's Detachment fly to Germany in October during deployment to Saudi Arabia. They traveled with four pickups and water purification equipment.

RON GARRISON
Lexington Herald-Leader

Bonita Mathis of the Georgia National Guard says good-bye to family members as her bus parades down Cherry Street in Macon, Ga. Her unit was headed to Ft. Stewart, Ga.

JAMES BORCHUCK
Macon Telegraph

Left:

A member of the 132nd Military Police National Guard unit from Florence, S.C., unloads equipment as the unit arrives at its first base in eastern Saudi Arabia in October. The unit traveled 45 hours and had to unpack before getting any rest.

JAMIE FRANCIS
The State, Columbia, S.C.

Below:

Mike Hanson makes his destination known as he arrives at Saddam Hussein International Airport in Baghdad in early December. He was in Kuwait when Iraq invaded and had been in hiding until the Iraqi president allowed all hostages to leave.

PAULINE LUBENS
Detroit Free Press

Soldiers from the Army's 101st Airborne Division carry on a traditional pastime near the Saudi-Iraqi border in January. Members of the 101st were among the first troops President George Bush ordered to the Mideast in early August.

DAVID C. TURNLEY
Detroit Free Press

Below:

Members of the 101st Airborne Division staked a geographic claim for their temporary home in the Saudi desert.

DAVID C. TURNLEY
Detroit Free Press

Right:

Matthew Armstrong of Grosse Pointe, Mich., a member of the 3rd Marine Division, shaves in the heat of the Saudi desert. His unit had no running water or tents until late December, but the members were required to shave daily.

TODD BUCHANAN
Philadelphia Inquirer

A member of the 101st Airborne Division staffs a bunker in Saudi Arabia just south of the Iraqi border in January.

DAVID C. TURNLEY
Detroit Free Press

Members of Iraq's People's Volunteer Army train on a Baghdad soccer field. After the invasion of Kuwait, Iraqi officials said thousands of civilians volunteered; when the war broke out, U.S. officials estimated Iraq had 545,000 troops in Kuwait and southern Iraq.

DAVID C. TURNLEY
Detroit Free Press

Members of the Army's 101st Airborne Division wear their gas masks as they wait on an airstrip near Dhahran, Saudi Arabia, for a flight to an area near the Iraqi border as a prelude to the air war.

DAVID C. TURNLEY
Detroit Free Press

**Marine Lance Cpl. Edgar
Johnson, left, and Lance Cpl.
Oliver Thomas catch up on the
news while waiting to take part
in a training exercise in eastern
Saudi Arabia in November. The
marines, who had been in Saudi
Arabia for three months, said
they seldom saw more than one
paper a week.**

JAMIE FRANCIS
The State, Columbia, S.C.

Two cooks warm up over a boiling pot near the Saudi-Iraqi border in January. Although most soldiers received hot food at least occasionally, many troops heading into battle and some others received MREs – rations called Meals Ready-to-Eat.

DAVID C. TURNLEY
Detroit Free Press

Below:

**A Kuwaiti army instructor
disciplines a volunteer during
field training in eastern Saudi
Arabia in November. The camp
trained volunteers for the
offensive to retake their
homeland.**

JAMIE FRANCIS
The State, Columbia, S.C.

Kuwaiti volunteers drill for ground fighting in eastern Saudi Arabia in late December. There were 1,200 exiles training in this encampment; more drilled in the United States. Kuwaiti troops were among the first into Kuwait City after the ground war began.

TODD BUCHANAN
Philadelphia Inquirer

Left:

Sabah Jabril, 15, peers out from a window in her tent at a Red Crescent refugee camp near Azrac, Jordan. Jabril, from Somalia, fled after Iraq's invasion of Kuwait and had been living in the camp along with 136 other Somalians.

PAULINE LUBENS
Detroit Free Press

Below:

Darryl Barnes, a member of the 2/2 Armored Cavalry Regiment, waits on a bus after arriving in eastern Saudi Arabia from Germany in early December. He and fellow soldiers were loaded onto the bus without being told their destination.

JAMIE FRANCIS
The State, Columbia, S.C.

Left:

On the day of the United Nations deadline, San Francisco police wrestle with a protester outside a federal building. Around the country, thousands of antiwar demonstrators marched; more than 500 people were arrested in San Francisco.

LLOYD FRANCIS JR.
San Jose Mercury News

Below:

The war also evoked powerful emotions for its supporters: Jim Booth, a Korean War veteran, shows a photo of his son, David, and daughter-in-law, Chong, to an antiwar protester during a rally in Boulder, Colo. David was a member of the Army.

EUGENE TANNER
Boulder Daily Camera

Left:

Pat Westberry, left, watches television reports on the outbreak of war on Jan. 16 in San Pedro, Calif., with Melissa Perez, 10, and Patti Utz. Westberry's husband and son were serving in the Persian Gulf.

CHRISTINA SALVADOR
Long Beach Press-Telegram

Below:

The Rev. Ferne Wolfe of Axemann United Methodist Church in Axemann, Pa., is among the members of the clergy to tell their congregations to have courage in the first days of the war.

DICK BROWN
Centre Daily Times

Coffins await at an air base in eastern Saudi Arabia.

SUSAN WINTERS
Philadelphia Daily News

Below:

A soldier sips coffee to warm himself in the cold early morning desert air at a forward refueling base in northern Saudi Arabia.

DAVID C. TURNLEY
Detroit Free Press

Right:

At a candlelight vigil at a plaza in Longmont, Colo., north of Denver, about 70 people sing and pray for peace. The theme of the vigil was "no blood for oil."

CLIFF GRASSMICK
Boulder Daily Camera

SCHWARZKOPF

The first time Gen. H. Norman Schwarzkopf stepped to the news conference podium in Riyadh, Saudi Arabia, a star was born, a four-star general of a star, a mythical military figure come to life. Though he wasn't old enough to fight in World War II, there was much of that war in the man – big and square in his unadorned fatigues, plain-spoken, close-cropped, unaffected.

But there was much of the modern media-trained executive, too, and the combination made him an instant hero with the public, if not the press, whom he regularly deflected, derided and dismayed from that podium at allied headquarters.

For the major media, he was prime interview material, and he sat with them all, reassuring, sentimental, tough, soft. He made no mistakes, it seemed, at least not until the fighting was over, when he told interviewer David Frost that he thought the war should have gone on longer than the president allowed. He soon apologized for that, and the president called to say all was forgiven.

Some said he ought to run for president himself. Schwarzkopf, having demonstrated how much he favors holding down losses and being sure of victory, was noncommittal.

The topic is Gen. H. Norman Schwarzkopf, the U.S. commander in the gulf. His friend Gen. Ward LeHardy said, "Norm is this generation's Doug MacArthur. He's got the tactical brilliance of Patton, the strategic insight of Eisenhower and the modesty of Bradley." Shortly after the war, President George Bush said of him and Gen. Colin Powell, chairman of the Joint Chiefs of Staff: "I don't know what they want to do, but they're big enough to do anything they want to do."

DAVID C. TURNLEY
Detroit Free Press

Below:

A bodyguard escorts Schwarzkopf as he arrives to encourage members of the 24th Infantry Division in eastern Saudi Arabia on Jan. 14. "Are you ready?" he shouted to one detachment. "Yes sir!" they hollered.

DAVID C. TURNLEY
Detroit Free Press

Right:

Schwarzkopf huddles with members of a Patriot missile battery outside Riyadh, Saudi Arabia, in late January. He called the soldiers "true American heroes."

DAVID C. TURNLEY
Detroit Free Press

THE STORM BEGINS

"Now that the war has started, we work about 20 hours a day. At night it looks like the Fourth of July. You're right, people just don't know how to get along.... Don't worry. I don't plan to get killed."

Pvt. Denny Hine, St. Augustine, Fla., to fifth-graders, Fairfield Elementary School, Ft. Wayne, Ind.

The Persian Gulf War began in the flame of allied fighter jets scorching the dark sky of Jan. 16. It announced itself to Saddam Hussein moments later in the fire of high explosives and the tracers of Baghdad's anti-aircraft artillery. The air war continued for 39 days — an eternity of devastation against which Iraqi defenses could do almost nothing.

The best counter-weapon Saddam Hussein could muster was a lumbering, unguided missile as unsophisticated as the allied weapons were advanced. But those Scud missiles falling on Israel and Saudi Arabia were to present a maddening threat, not just to the victims below, but to the delicate diplomacy that had brought a phalanx of Arab nations to cooperate with the other allies against an Arab aggressor. Hussein hoped the Scuds would bring Israel into the war, shattering that Arab commitment and possibly the allied war effort.

The allies responded to the Scuds with Patriot missiles, with repeated calls for forebearance from Israel and with an intense air search for elusive, mobile Scud launchers that stretched the air war well beyond its original timetable.

In the end, the most destructive Scud attack occurred not in Israel but in Saudi Arabia, as a warhead plunged into a barracks of Americans who had arrived only days before. Twenty-eight died.

An F15 takes off at dusk during the first day of the air war from the USS John F. Kennedy in the Red Sea. On the deck are A7 bombers.

TODD BUCHANAN
Philadelphia Inquirer

Previous page:

A crew completes the process of loading a 1,000-pound gravity bomb under the wing of an A6 bomber on the deck of the aircraft carrier USS Theodore Roosevelt in the Persian Gulf in early February.

TODD BUCHANAN
Philadelphia Inquirer

Below:

A High Speed Anti-Radiation Missile on the wing of a fighter is checked on the USS John F. Kennedy early in the war. The missiles, which seek and destroy radar installations, were used against Iraqi Scud missile sites.

TODD BUCHANAN
Philadelphia Inquirer

Right:

The deck crew of the Kennedy prepares an F14 Tomcat in the Red Sea during the first week of the allied air campaign.

TODD BUCHANAN
Philadelphia Inquirer

Smoke rises from downtown Tel Aviv, Israel, after an Iraqi Scud missile hit on Jan. 19. Before the war, Iraq threatened to make Tel Aviv one of its first targets if attacked; it carried out those threats within the first days.

MICHAEL RONDOU
San Jose Mercury News

Left:

Residents examine the wreckage after a Scud missile attack Feb. 9 on a residential area of Tel Aviv. The neighborhood was home to many Iraqi Jews. No one was killed in the attack, but 26 people were hurt.

JON KRAL
Miami Herald

Below:

Orna Kritzman, 60, prays for safety after a Scud destroyed a textile factory about 200 yards from her home in Azor, Israel, a suburb of Tel Aviv, on Jan. 18. The missile, which hit about 2:15 a.m., blew out the windows and doors of many area homes.

MICHAEL RONDOU
San Jose Mercury News

Workers examine the rubble of a house in Tel Aviv destroyed by an Iraqi Scud missile. The residents, who had gone to a bomb shelter, were not injured in the Jan. 23 attack. Israeli officials vowed to retaliate for Scud attacks, but did not.

JON KRAL
Miami Herald

Left:

Patriot missiles rise from Riyadh, Saudi Arabia, to intercept an Iraqi Scud. Iraq launched about 85 Scuds; about 50 were intercepted by Patriots, although warheads or debris sometimes fell and caused damage.

AKIRA SUWA
Philadelphia Inquirer

Below:

A billboard instructs residents of Dammam, Saudi Arabia, how to protect themselves. People throughout the Mideast took precautions against chemical or biological weapons, but despite Saddam Hussein's threats, no Scuds carried them.

AKIRA SUWA
Philadelphia Inquirer

طرق الوقايه من غازات الحروب الكيماوية
Safegards against chemical war gases.

الاتجاه الى اقرب مكان آمن ومغلق
(منزل - دكان ..... الخ)
Run to the nearest safe & closed place e.g. house. shop etc.

تغطية الرأس بأي شيئ في متناول اليد
وضع الايدي في الجيوب
Cover your head Put your hands in your pockets.

تواجدك في الشارع
IN STREET

غلق الابواب والنوافذ وجميع الفتحات
ومراوح شفط الهواء بأحكام
Close all doors & windows & seal all opening & exhaust fans securely.

فتح المذياع أو التلفاز للاستماع وتلقي
تعليمات الدفاع المدني
Listen to the radio or T.V. to receive Civil Defense instructions.

تواجدك في المنزل
IN HOUSE

مع تحيات : البنك الأهلي التجاري و قيادة الدفاع المدني بالمنطقة الشرقية

Below:

Kathy Derderian, a student at Wayne State University in Detroit, protests the outbreak of the war the day after it started. About 50 protesters entered a campus building chanting "What do we want? U.S. out! When do we want it? Now!"

WILLIAM ARCHIE
Detroit Free Press

Right:

Nitzan Maas, 3, holds hands with her father, Yiftach, of Farmington Hills, Mich., during a pro-Israel rally at Congregation Shaarey Zedek on Jan. 27. About 2,000 people attended the rally to show support for U.S.-Israeli solidarity.

CRAIG PORTER
Detroit Free Press

The barber is
IN

Come in and if I'm not to busy
I'll cut your hair now. If I am
busy I'll tell you when you can
come back.

REAL-LIFE MASH

The heroic image of battle-hardened, sentimental military medics stanching the blood of war was part of combat lore long before the movie and the TV series made "MASH" a cherished piece of American culture. The men and women of the 5th Mobile Army Surgical Hospital revived that legend and that reality once more in south-central Iraq, in a cluster of tents set up to treat the war's most seriously wounded, in a hurry.

In anticipation of the life-giving, emergency-room chaos to come, they had waited long weeks, preparing logistically and mentally for the worst of the war. As allied troops and tanks rolled across the Saudi border into Iraq, they would move in, too, along with the 24th Mechanized Infantry Division.

The way the war went, they treated more Iraqis than allies. There was more sympathy than contempt toward the defeated Iraqis; decisions favoring wounded Iraqis over less seriously injured Americans were made with fast, neutral professionalism. There would be time for personal feelings, for reflection about this war and its victims, but only when the shooting stopped.

Previous page

Before the ground war began, the members of the 5th Mobile Army Surgical Hospital did their best to make their temporary camp near the Saudi-Iraqi border feel like home. A dentist sits for a trim from a nurse who doubled as the camp barber.

DAVID C. TURNLEY
Detroit Free Press

Below, left:

On the last day before the ground war began, Dr. Nelson Wiegman, a surgeon, writes a letter to his wife in North Carolina. He had not seen her for six months.

DAVID C. TURNLEY
Detroit Free Press

Below, right:

A soldier from another unit visits the MASH camp to see his wife, one of the unit's nurses.

DAVID C. TURNLEY
Detroit Free Press

Following page:

With the ground war hours away, MASH unit members get in some aerobics in the afternoon sun. Once the offensive began, the unit moved into southern Iraq with soldiers from the Army's 24th Mechanized Infantry Division.

DAVID C. TURNLEY
Detroit Free Press

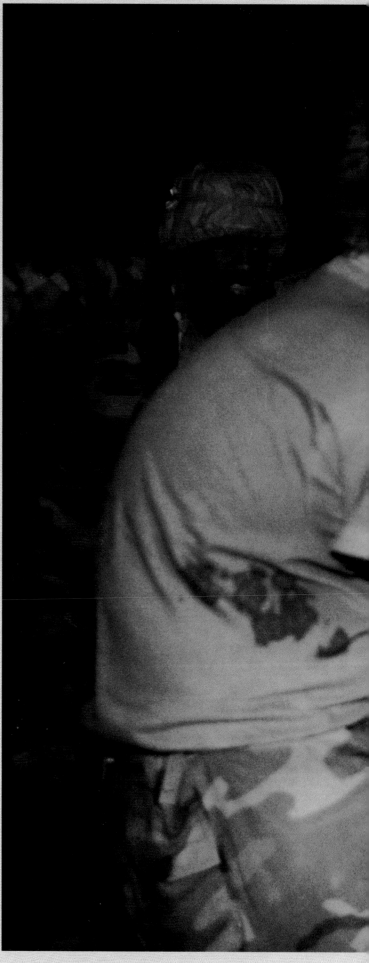

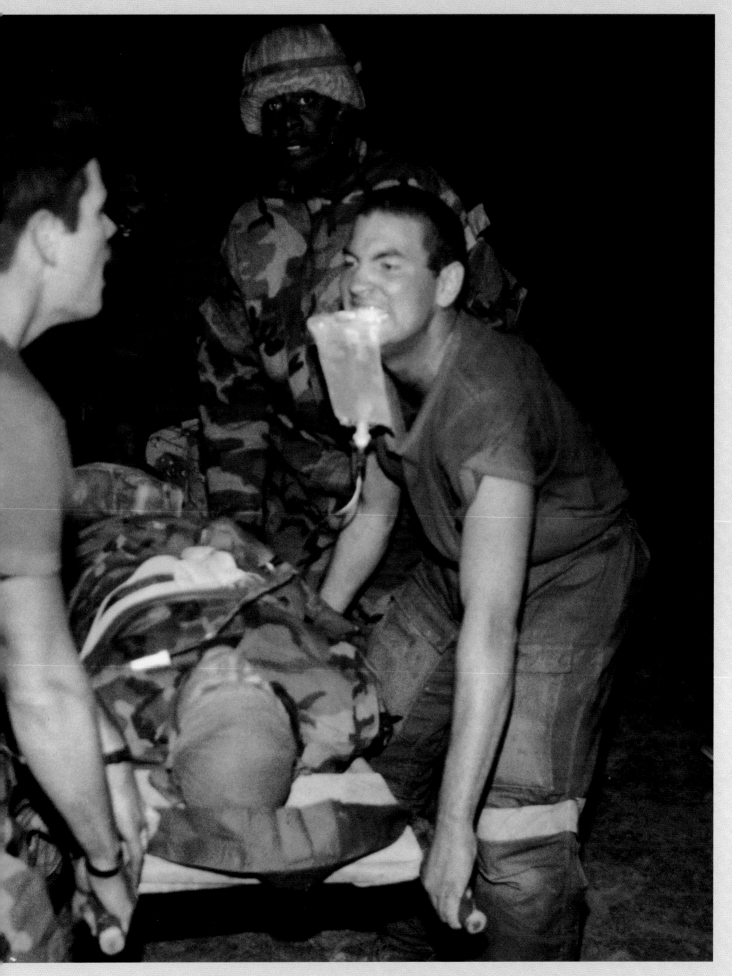

Surgeons study a wounded soldier's X rays near the battlefield.

DAVID C. TURNLEY
Detroit Free Press

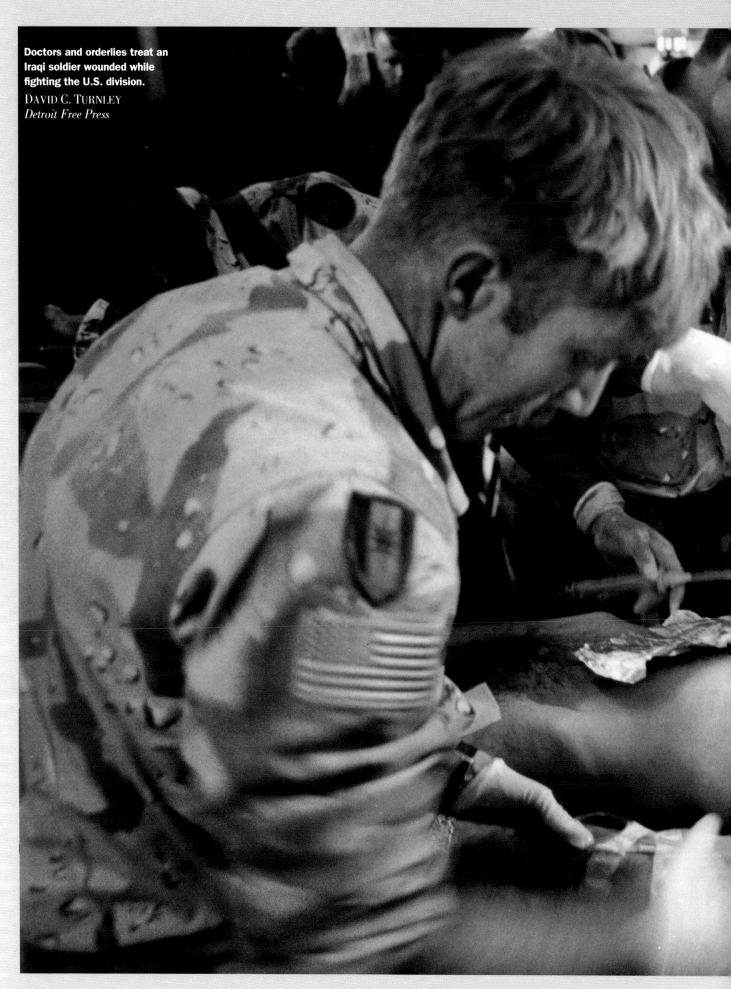

Doctors and orderlies treat an Iraqi soldier wounded while fighting the U.S. division.
DAVID C. TURNLEY
Detroit Free Press

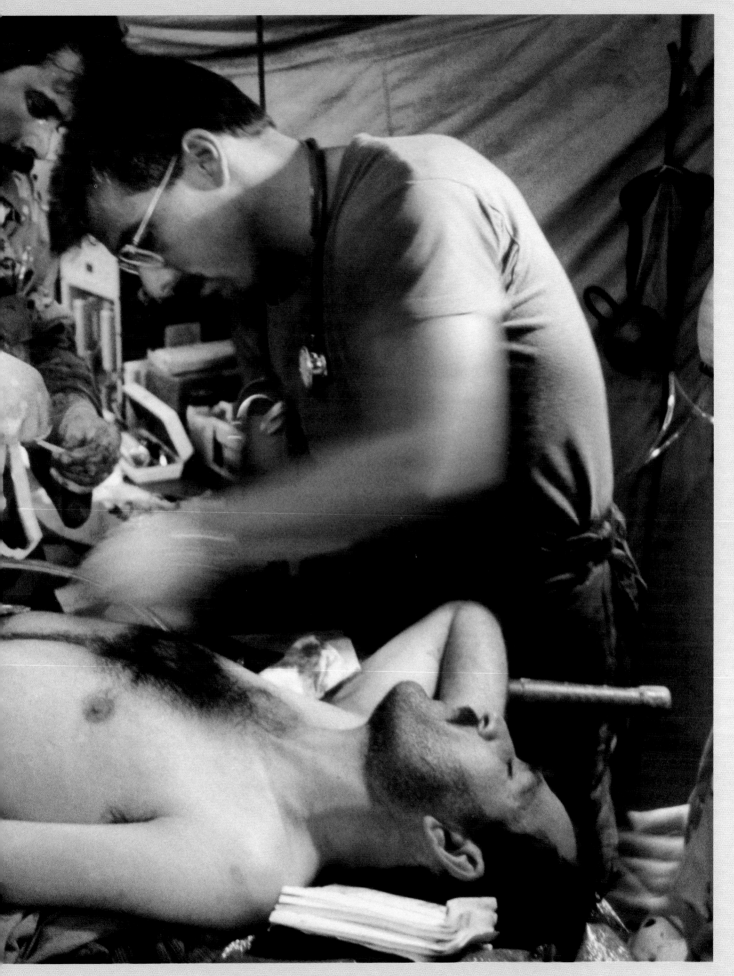

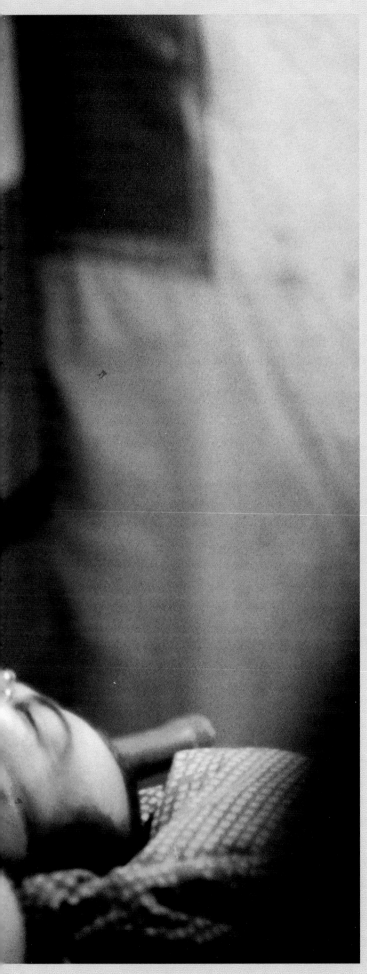

Marines from the 2nd Division approach a foxhole with Iraqi soldiers holding up leaflets to surrender in southern Kuwait in the first hours of the ground war.

TODD BUCHANAN
Philadelphia Inquirer

100 HOURS

"We're focused, eager, confident and alert, as well as missing home, worried, scared and optimistic – not knowing what the future may hold. The soldier or person who says he wants to go fight, and is not afraid, is someone who belongs in a mental institution."

Army Spec. Jeffrey Desein, Woolridge, Ohio.

The ground war loomed so ominously that some people hoped and prayed until the last that it might be avoidable. When it finally happened, Gen. H. Norman Schwarzkopf's "Hail Mary" sweep of soldiers, tanks and artillery around the west flank of the Iraqi army ordained how the land battle would end almost before it started.

Outmaneuvered and outgunned, the Iraqis ran out of white things to wave in surrender. Iraqi armored vehicles were destroyed by the hundreds, and many men died.

This was not a war of epic confrontation, of frontline ebb and flow. Images of tremendous all-out battle were scarce. This was a rout, and it looked that way.

The one-sidedness of the final fighting made each death more poignant, each Iraqi death one more tick on a counter running high into the tens of thousands, each allied death one more example that the random lightning strikes of war find even the victors.

Below, top:

Sgt. Larry Williams rides through the breach in the Iraqi lines as the 2nd Marine Division moves into Kuwait in the early morning of the ground war's first day.

TODD BUCHANAN
Philadelphia Inquirer

Below, bottom:

A marine asks an Iraqi prisoner how many other soldiers are in the bunker he just left. The bunker was part of the headquarters of the 14th Iraqi Infantry Division.

TODD BUCHANAN
Philadelphia Inquirer

Below:

Iraqi vehicles smoulder along a highway in Kuwait after the cease-fire had been declared. The Iraqi convoy was retreating when it was hit by allied air and artillery attacks.

TODD BUCHANAN
Philadelphia Inquirer

Troops remove casualties from a
Bradley Fighting Vehicle during
an intense battle between
members of the 24th
Mechanized Infantry Division
and the Iraqi Republican Guard
near the Euphrates River in Iraq.

DAVID C. TURNLEY
Detroit Free Press

**Soldiers evacuate. They said the
vehicle was hit by fire from an
Army M1 tank.**

DAVID C. TURNLEY
Detroit Free Press

Ken Kozakiewicz, 23, center, is
helped by an evacuation crew to
a helicopter after being wounded
when the Bradley Fighting
Vehicle was hit.
DAVID C. TURNLEY
Detroit Free Press

Ken Kozakiewicz comforts
Michael Tsantarakis, of Queens,
N.Y., who was also injured. After
the driver of the vehicle is
placed into the helicopter,
Kozakiewicz reacts when he
realizes that his friend has been
killed.

DAVID C. TURNLEY
Detroit Free Press

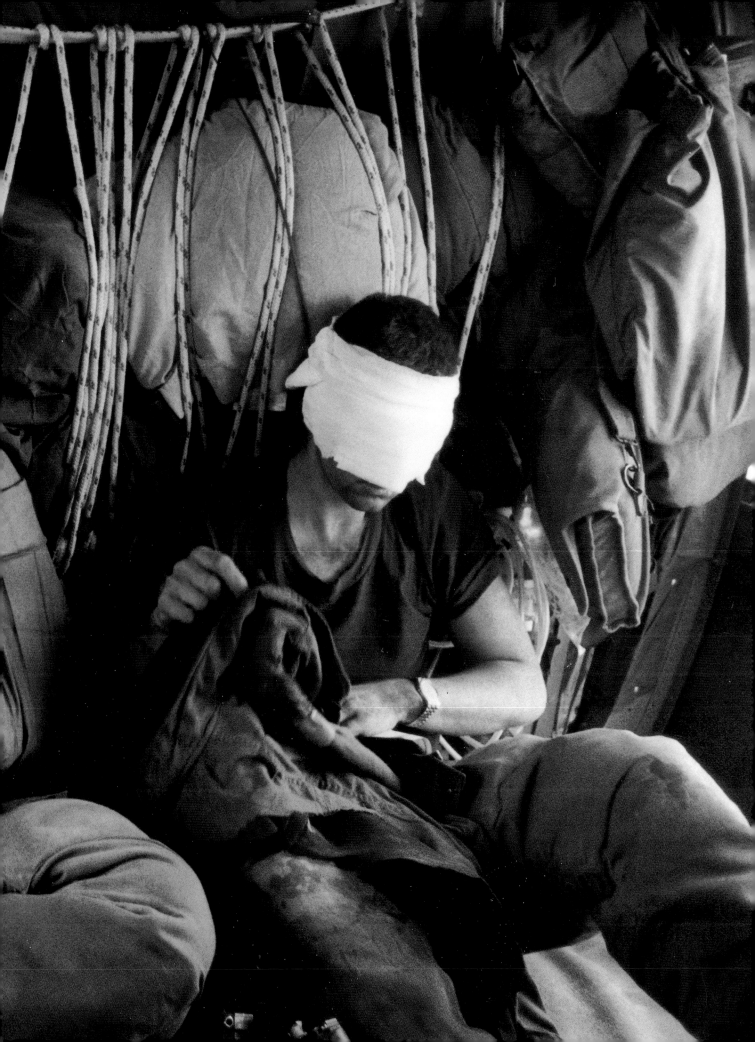

A U.S. soldier examines a truck that was hit in southern Iraq on Highway 8 between Kuwait and Baghdad during the final days of the war. Although there were no official estimates of Iraqi casualties, the number is believed to be in the tens of thousands.

DAVID C. TURNLEY
Detroit Free Press

Below:

Kuwaitis take stock of their capital after allied forces retook it on Feb. 27 after months of Iraqi occupation.

TODD BUCHANAN
Philadelphia Inquirer

Right:

Iraqi family members peer through the back of their truck after crossing through a U.S. Army checkpoint just north of the Kuwaiti border. The family of farmers had gone to another village, looking for food.

PAULINE LUBENS
Detroit Free Press

Below:

U.S. soldiers walk by an Iraqi casualty on the highway linking Basra, Iraq, and Kuwait City shortly after the cease-fire was declared.

TODD BUCHANAN
Philadelphia Inquirer

Right:

At the Iraqi border, Kuwaiti children on a donkey survey a damaged tank abandoned on the side of the road during Iraq's retreat from Kuwait.

DAVID C. TURNLEY
Detroit Free Press

Following page:

Marine Cpl. Matt Robbins of Hallowell, Maine, is greeted by Kuwaitis outside the U.S. Embassy on the day Kuwait City was liberated. His elite 2nd Force Reconnaissance Company retook the embassy the day before the full liberation.

TODD BUCHANAN
Philadelphia Inquirer

Below:

Marines from the company raise the American flag inside the embassy compound. They found a flag already flying when they arrived, so they raised theirs on the vehicle antenna. The prisoners were captured by Kuwaiti resistance fighters.

TODD BUCHANAN
Philadelphia Inquirer

Right:

Kuwaitis fly their flag in celebration of Kuwait City's liberation.

TODD BUCHANAN
Philadelphia Inquirer

Members of the 2nd Marine Division combat engineers pose with a portrait of Saddam Hussein before destroying it. The mosaic was on the outskirts of Kuwait City; the soldiers' order to blow it up later was rescinded, so it was bulldozed.

TODD BUCHANAN
Philadelphia Inquirer

IT'S OVER

"After living in this hole for so long, home with you will be heaven.... To talk and see you at the same time. To reach out and feel your cheek.... To kiss you and hold you in my arms. That is to be home."

Sgt. 1C Danny Hayden, Hinesville, Ga., to his wife Jane.

It hadn't been a long war, but it had been a long, anxious wait, and so the reunions were just as ardent as if the fighting had lasted years, and the country was just as welcoming. At air bases across the land, huge crowds gathered to welcome home spouses and friends and heroic strangers, and in homes in every town, the yellow ribbons seemed to have turned from pale and wistful to proud and bright.

There were tragic returns – 333 men and women sent home to be buried, thousands more destined to cope indefinitely with life-changing injuries, a Virginia military mother whose young son had been abducted and murdered while she was away, a Michigan soldier murdered as he was packing to move in Detroit. But most came home relieved and triumphant, to relieved and loving arms, heroes and heroines just for going and coming back, however much or little they did during the war.

So unlike their predecessors in Vietnam, they had served their country's image as well as its interests and left it feeling good – about them, about itself.

An unidentified soldier leaps into the arms of a fellow soldier from the 311th Evacuation Hospital unit after it landed at Volk Field near Ft. McCoy, Wis. The March 12 celebration marked the first return of North Dakotans from the war.

ERIC HYLDEN
Grand Forks (N.D.) Herald

Left:

Pvt. Ken Thames of Kingstree, S.C., greets well-wishers on his return to his home state.

ANNE McGUARY
The State, Columbia, S.C.

Below:

Kwang Suk Hitt reacts to the arrival of her husband, Sgt. 1C Peter Hitt, and other members of the 101st Airborne Division as their plane arrives at Ft. Campbell, Ky., on March 9. It was the first 101st Airborne troops to arrive at the base.

RON GARRISON
Lexington Herald-Leader

Ed Loupe of Louisiana helps carry the casket of Cpl. James Miller to its grave in Decatur, Ind. Miller was killed in Iraq on Feb. 28 when he stepped on a land mine; Loupe was about 40 feet from him. They had become best friends while they were stationed in Germany.

KEITH HITCHENS
Ft. Wayne News-Sentinel

Right:

Army Staff Sgt. Daniel Stamaris Jr., of Boise, Idaho, salutes from his stretcher at Andrews Air Force Base in Maryland on March 10. Stamaris, who had been listed as missing in action, took part in ceremonies honoring returning MIAs and prisoners of war.

RICK BOWMER
Philadelphia Inquirer

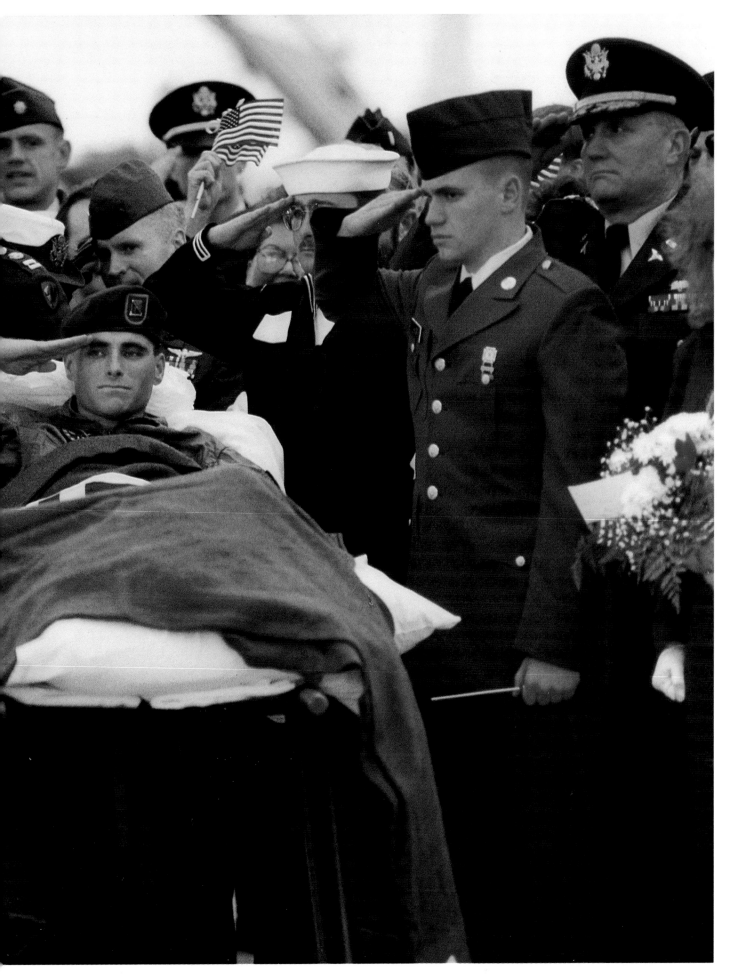

Left:

A boy hands a flag to a marine at Norton Air Force Base in California. About 250 people welcomed them; one of them, Vietnam veteran Col. Buck Bedard, said the welcome was important "especially for those of us who served in Vietnam."

THOMAS VAN DYKE
San Jose Mercury News

Below:

Jordanians carry a mockup of a Scud missile and wave Iraqi flags in support of Iraqi President Saddam Hussein during a march in Amman the day the cease-fire was declared. More than 5,000 people chanted in praise of Hussein.

AKIRA SUWA
Philadelphia Inquirer

Crowds wait for returning prisoner of war Air Force Maj. Jeffrey Tice March 10 at Andrews Air Force Base in Maryland. Tice said he was beaten and given electric shocks during captivity. "You kind of got numb after the first few shocks," he said. "It sounds bad, but it wasn't that terrible."

TOM MIHALEK
Philadelphia Daily News

Returning POWs salute after landing. They are, from left, Air Force Capt. William Andrews, Navy lieutenants Jeffrey Zaun, Lawrence Slade and Robert Wetzel. In all, 21 Americans were held as prisoners. Zaun was among those forced to make a statement on Iraqi television denouncing the war.

G. LOIE GROSSMANN
Philadelphia Daily News

President George Bush greets Air Force Capt. Spike Thomas during a homecoming celebration at Sumter, S.C., on March 17. Bush told the troops: "You know, you all not only helped liberate Kuwait. You helped this country liberate itself from old ghosts and doubts."

JIM ARNOLD
The State, Columbia, S.C.

Air Force Capt. Steven Tate snaps a picture of his 4-year-old son, Patrick, during his daughter's birthday party in March at the family's home in Hampton, Va. Tate's wife, Valerie, and daughter, Melissa, 2, are in the background. Tate was credited with shooting down the first Iraqi plane during the war.

JESSICA GREENE
Detroit Free Press

EPILOGUE

In a war provoked largely by lust for oil, oil flowed free in the once-clean waters of the Persian Gulf, oil soaked the ground of the Arabian Desert like earth's blood, and oil burned uncontainably from hundreds of Kuwaiti wells sabotaged by the armies of Iraq.

The wealth of Kuwait was going up in smoke at the rate of $100 million a day, and the best oil fire fighters in the world said some of the fires would burn for several years.

Oil had made Kuwait, Iraq and Saudi Arabia. First it made them targets of Western colonialism and corporate exploitation. Then it made them nations of power and plenty. Then, perhaps inevitably, it made them battlegrounds. What it will make of them next no one can say, but for months, perhaps for years after the Persian Gulf War has become a receding six-week episode in the region's turbulent history, that signature of smoke in the sky will hang for all three countries and the rest of the world to see, a reminder of the possibilities.

Above, top:

Iraqi troops ignited hundreds of oil wells in Kuwait; fire fighters estimated some would burn for years.

Above:

The environment was a major casualty. Millions of gallons of oil fouled the Persian Gulf in January before U.S. bombing missions stanched the flow.

TODD BUCHANAN
Philadelphia Inquirer

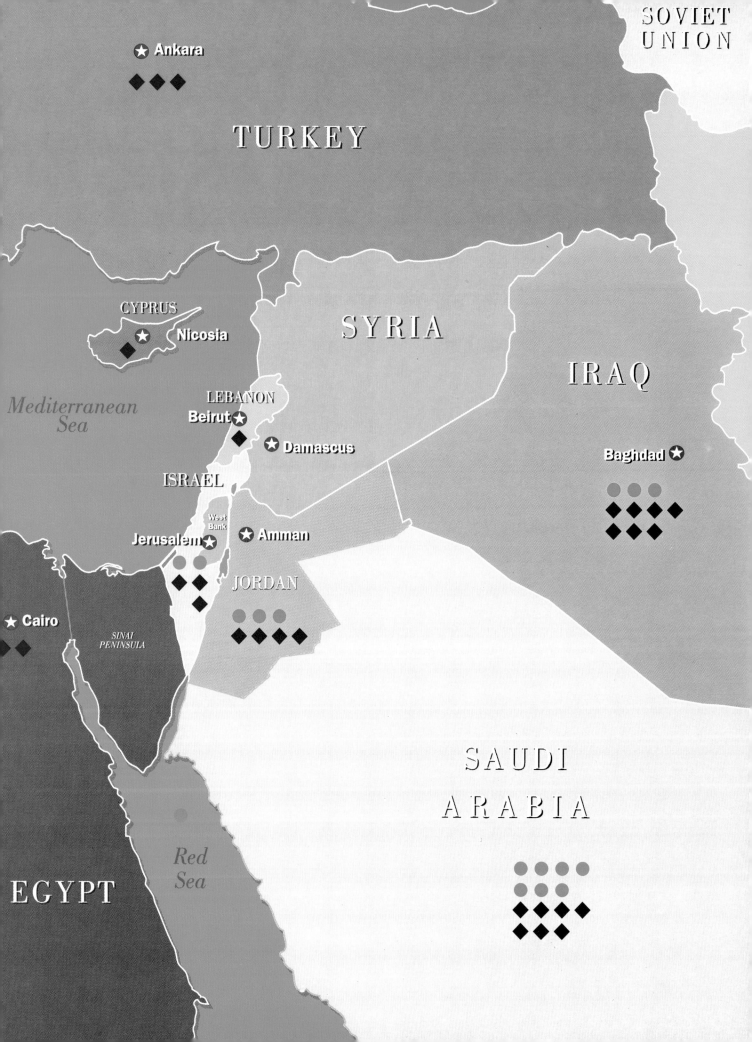

SOVIET
UNION

★ Ankara
◆◆◆

TURKEY

CYPRUS
★ Nicosia
◆

*Mediterranean
Sea*

SYRIA

IRAQ

LEBANON
Beirut ★
◆
★ Damascus

Baghdad ★
●●●
◆◆◆◆
◆◆◆

ISRAEL

West
Bank
Jerusalem ★
★ Amman
●●
◆◆
◆
JORDAN
●●●
◆◆◆◆

★ Cairo
◆◆

*SINAI
PENINSULA*

SAUDI
ARABIA

*Red
Sea*

EGYPT

●●●●
●●●
◆◆◆◆
◆◆◆

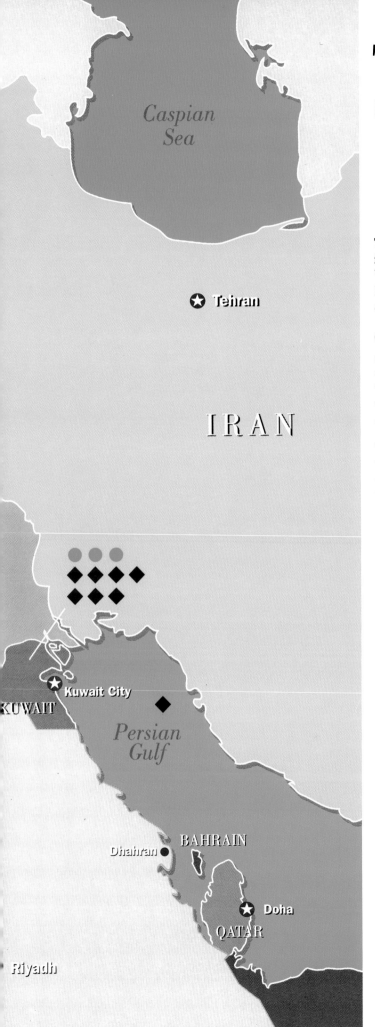

THE PERSIAN GULF

These 21 photographers and reporters covered the war for Knight-Ridder. They were organized through Clark Hoyt, Washington Bureau Chief. Besides this group, various Knight-Ridder newspapers sent additional staff to provide further coverage for their own areas.

● PHOTOGRAPHERS

Charlie Borst
KRTN
Saudi Arabia

Todd Buchanan
Philadelphia Inquirer
Iraq, Kuwait, Saudi Arabia, Red Sea

Jamie Francis
The State, Columbia, S.C.
Saudi Arabia

Tom Gralish
Philadelphia Inquirer
Saudi Arabia

Jon Kral
Miami Herald
Israel

Pauline Lubens
Detroit Free Press
Iraq, Jordan, Kuwait

Michael Rondou
San Jose Mercury News
Israel

Akira Suwa
Philadelphia Inquirer
Jordan, Saudi Arabia

David Turnley
Detroit Free Press
Iraq, Jordan, Kuwait, Saudi Arabia

◆ REPORTERS

Frank Bruni
Detroit Free Press
Iraq, Kuwait, Saudi Arabia

Larry Copeland
Philadelphia Inquirer
Iraq, Kuwait, Saudi Arabia

Tom Fiedler
Miami Herald
Iraq, Kuwait, Saudi Arabia

Vernon Loeb
Philadelphia Inquirer
Israel, Jordan

Pat May
Miami Herald
Iraq, Kuwait, Saudi Arabia, Turkey

Marty Merzer
Miami Herald
Israel, Jordan

Carol Morello
Philadelphia Inquirer
Iraq, Kuwait, Saudia Arabia, Persian Gulf

Carol Rosenberg
Miami Herald
Iraq, Israel, Jordan, Kuwait, Saudi Arabia

Peter Slevin
Philadelphia Inquirer
Cypress, Egypt, Turkey

Juan Tamayo
Miami Herald
Iraq, Kuwait, Saudi Arabia

Remer Tyson
Detroit Free Press
Egypt, Turkey

Jocelyne Zablit
Detroit Free Press
Egypt, Jordan, Lebanon

BIOGRAPHIES

William Archie

William Archie was born in Detroit and has been a Free Press staff photographer since 1979. He graduated from Wayne State University in 1981 with a bachelor's degree in fine arts. He's studied Spanish at Wayne State and in Mexico and Spain.

Photo: Page 98.

Jim Arnold

Jim Arnold has worked at the State in Columbia, S.C., since 1990. He has also worked at the State Journal-Register in Springfield, Ill., and graduated from Ohio University.

Photo: Pages 146-147.

Patricia Beck

Patricia Beck joined the Detroit Free Press as a photographer in 1977. She is a 1975 graduate with honors from Ohio University with a bachelor of science degree in journalism, with a major in photojournalism.

A native metropolitan Detroiter, she has received several awards for photography including having several of her prints in the permanent contemporary photography collection at the Bibliotheque Nationale in Paris.

Photos: Pages 23, 24-25.

James Borchuck

James Borchuck has worked at the Macon Telegraph since February 1990. He graduated from Western Kentucky University in 1989,

Akira Suwa and Todd Buchanan

and won fourth place in that year's William Randolph Hearst competition. He has worked at the Ogden Standard-Examiner in Utah, the Bay City Times and Lansing State Journal in Michigan, the Orlando Sentinel and Cincinnati Enquirer.

Pages 45, 48-49.

Rick Bowman

Philadelphia Inquirer
Photo: Pages 140-141.

Dick Brown

Centre Daily Times
Photo: Page 73.

Todd Buchanan

Todd Buchanan, 29, joined the staff of the Philadelphia Inquirer in 1990 after working for three years at the Courier-Journal in Louisville, Ky. He also had been a photographer

at the Orange County Register, where he was part of the team that won a Pulitzer Prize for spot news photography for coverage of the 1984 Los Angeles Summer Olympics.

Buchanan, a 1983 photo-journalism graduate of Western Kentucky University, has also worked for the National Geographic Society photography department and the Des Moines Register and Tribune.

He spent three months in the Persian Gulf area, covering the prewar buildup, the beginning of the air war from the Red Sea, and the U.S. marines in Kuwait.

Photos: Pages 10-11, 26, 28, 29, 31, 32-33, 54-55, 63, 82-83, 84-85, 86, 87, 88-89, 114-115, 116, 116-117, 126-127, 128-129, 130-131, 132, 132-133, 134-135, 151.

Tim Dominick

Tim Dominick has worked for the State newspaper in Columbia, S.C., for three years. Dominick, a graduate of Randolph Community College in Asheboro, N.C., has also worked at the Columbia Record and Charlotte Observer.

Photo: Pages 14-15.

Tom Ervin

Tom Ervin has been a photojournalist for nine years, the last three at The News in Boca Raton, Fla. He also worked for the Palm Beach Post and as a salesman, in factories and on road crews. He has covered the Mexico City earthquake and AIDS victims and their families. He spent one year documenting an Alzheimer's disease treatment facility.

Photos: Pages 40-41, 41.

Jamie Francis

Jamie Francis, 28, was born in the Blue Ridge mountains of North Carolina. He is a 1985 graduate of the University of North Carolina at Chapel Hill, with a degree in journalism. He paid for college by working at the Durham Herald Co. papers in North Carolina.

After graduation, he worked for three years at the Virginian-Pilot in Norfolk, Va., and moved to Columbia, S.C., in August 1990 to work at the State newspaper.

Photos: Pages 18, 46, 50-51, 60, 62, 64-65, 69.

Lloyd Francis Jr.

Lloyd Francis Jr. was born in Oakland, Calif., and raised in Hayward. He attended San Francisco State University. He began his journalism career at United Press International and interned at the Philadelphia Daily News and the Fresno (Calif.) Bee, where he was hired as a photographer in 1988. He has been a staff photographer at the San Jose Mercury News since 1990.

Photo: Pages 70-71.

Ron Garrison

Ron Garrison has been a photographer with the Lexington Herald-Leader since 1974. He graduated from the University of Kentucky in 1975 and has photographed in Haiti and Saudi Arabia, and enjoys covering the thoroughbred racing industry. He has been honored by the Kentucky Press Association, Kentucky News Photographers Association and Southern Photographers Association.

Photos: Pages 8-9, 47, 139.

Cliff Grassmick

Cliff Grassmick was born and reared in Rocky Ford, Colo. He began his photography career in high school, and pursued it when he traveled around the world on a ship with 500 students while attending the University of Colorado. He worked in counseling and mental health after receiving his degree in psychology and journalism and began to work at the Boulder Daily Camera three years ago.

Photos: Pages 20-21, 76-77.

Jessica Greene

Jessica Greene is a 1989 graduate of the University of Michigan, where she majored in anthropology. Greene grew up in Chevy Chase, Md. In 1987, she traveled through India, Thailand, Nepal and Japan teaching English and taking pictures. She was an intern at the Flint Journal in Michigan after graduation and an intern at the Detroit Free Press during the summer of

Jon Kral

1990. She is a staff photographer at Gannett Westchester Newspapers, in Westchester County, N.Y.

Photo: Pages 148-149.

G. Loie Grossmann

Philadelphia Daily News photographer G. Loie Grossmann free-lanced for several publications before going to work at the Daily News in 1983. She is a three-time winner of the New Jersey photographer of the year award and a 1976 journalism graduate of Pennsylvania State University.

Photo: Page 145.

Keith Hitchens

Ft. Wayne News-Sentinel
Photo: Page 140.

Allen Horne

Columbus Ledger-Enquirer
Photo: Pages 34-35.

Eric Hylden

Eric Hylden went to work for the Grand Forks Herald in 1986. He is a native North Dakotan who grew up on a farm

70 miles from Grand Forks. He has won several state and regional awards, and has served four terms as Dakota Press Photographers Association president.

Photo: Pages 136-137.

Grant Jeffries

Bradenton Herald
Photo: Pages 42-43.

Bob King

Bob King, chief photographer at the Duluth News-Tribune, moved to Minnesota from Illinois in 1979. He received a bachelor's degree in German languages from the University of Illinois, and enjoys travel, astronomy, walking and music.

Photo: Page 19.

Paul Kitagaki Jr.

Paul Kitagaki Jr. has always worked and lived in the San Francisco Bay area. He received a bachelor's in broadcasting, radio and television from San Francisco State University. He worked at the San Francisco Progress, the San Mateo Times and the San Francisco Examiner before moving to the San Jose Mercury News in 1987. He has won several awards for his photojournalism.

Photo: Page 42.

Jon Kral

Jon Kral, 45, was born in New Jersey and grew up in Florida. After working as a cinema photographer for CBS, he free-lanced for newspapers

Jamie Francis

around the world before going to work for the Palm Beach Post in 1980. He went to the Miami Herald in 1983.

He has been on assignment in Israel three times, including during the gulf crisis. He has won several awards from the National Press Photographers Association and Green Eyeshade.

Photos: Pages 92-93, 94-95.

Len Lahman

Len Lahman is assistant chief photographer for the San Jose Mercury News, a position he has held since 1982. He previously worked for the Los Angeles Times and four other newspapers. A graduate of the University of Missouri, Lahman won a first place in the 1981 Robert F. Kennedy journalism awards for his story on undocumented workers from Mexico.

Photo: Page 30.

Pauline Lubens

Detroit Free Press senior staff photographer Pauline Lubens, 35, was born in New York City. Raised in Dayton, Ohio, Lubens graduated from the University of Michigan in 1977 with a bachelor of arts degree in history.

She began her professional career at the Trenton (N.J.) Times and came to the Free Press in 1983. Lubens has photographed on assignment in the Middle East, the Summer Olympics in Seoul, South Korea, and throughout Eastern

Pauline Lubens

Europe. She was one of two newspaper photographers to cover the release of American hostages in Baghdad.

She was named Michigan Photographer of the Year in 1989, and won the Michigan Understanding Award in 1990 from the Michigan Press Photographers Association for a project on families who care for their aging parents.

Photos: Page 51, 68-69, 126.

Anne McGuary

The State, Columbia, S.C.
Photo: Pages 138-139.

Tom Mihalek

Tom Mihalek has been a freelance photographer with the Philadelphia Daily News since 1985. He received a bachelor's degree in documentary film production from Temple University and has spent more than 15 years photographing news in the Philadelphia area.

Photo: Page 144.

Craig Porter

Craig Porter has worked as a Detroit Free Press photographer since 1975, covering stories from Florida to the Yukon Territory. He grew up in northern Indiana and studied journalism and psychology at Michigan State University.

Photo: Pages 98-99.

Michael Rondou

Michael Rondou, 42, began his career in journalism at age 31 after working as a project planner for a manufacturer of oil drilling equipment.

He began his newspaper career at the Palm Springs Desert Sun. He also has worked at the Long Beach Press-Telegram and the Hartford Courant, and began working for the San Jose Mercury News in 1987.

The gulf war was not his first; he served as an infantryman in Vietnam in 1970.

Photos: Pages 17, 90-91, 93.

Michael Rondou

Cristina Salvador

Cristina Salvador joined the Long Beach Press-Telegram in 1988. She was an intern at the Detroit Free Press and Magnum Photos, and was a finalist for the Nikon Sabbatical in 1991. She graduated from the University of Missouri in 1986.

Photo: Pages 72-73.

Jeff Siner

Jeff Siner has been a staff photographer for the Charlotte Observer since January 1989. He attended Indiana University, where he majored in journalism and minored in psychology.

Photo: Pages 158-159.

Akira Suwa

Akira Suwa, 49, a citizen of Japan, was born in Taikyu, Korea, and grew up in Japan. He came to the United States in 1967, and began to work at the Tampa Tribune in 1970. He also worked at the St. Petersburg Times and Palm Beach Post before moving to the Philadelphia Inquirer in 1977.

He has photographed on assignment in Japan, Southeast Asia, Libya, France and England. He won the Overseas Press Club "Best Photographic Reporting from Abroad" award in 1986. In addition to National Headliners and World Press Photo awards, he was Florida Newspaper Photographer of the Year and National Press Photographers Associa-

156

tion Region 6 Photographer of the Year.

Photos: Pages 22, 96, 97, 143.

Eugene Tanner

Oregon State University graduate Eugene Tanner joined the Daily Camera staff in Boulder, Colo., in 1989. He also worked for the Los Angeles Times, Seattle Times, Maui News and Corvallis Gazette-Times in Oregon.

Photo: Page 71.

David C. Turnley

Paris-based photographer David C. Turnley, 35, was born in Indiana and has been a Detroit Free Press staff member since 1980. He won the Pulitzer Prize for feature photography in 1990 for photographs from China and Eastern Europe. He won the Overseas Press Club Robert Capa award in 1990 for his Eastern Europe coverage. Turnley was also the recipient of the World Press photo of the year award in 1988 for a picture from the Armenian earthquake.

Turnley graduated in 1977 from the University of Michigan with a bachelor of arts degree in French literature. He also studied at the Sorbonne in Paris.

Turnley is the author of "Why Are They Weeping," a book about South Africans under apartheid. He coauthored, with his brother Peter, "Beijing Spring," about the events in Tiananmen Square,

David C. Turnley

China, and "Moments of Revolution," pictures from Eastern Europe and the pro-democracy movement.

Photos: Cover, back cover, Pages 6-7, 12-13, 27, 38-39, 44, 52-53, 54, 56, 57, 58-59, 61, 76, 76-77, 78-79, 80, 81, 100-101, 102, 102-103, 104-105, 106, 106-107, 108-109, 110-111, 112-113, 113, 118, 119, 120-121, 122, 122-123, 124-125, 128.

Jeff Tuttle

Jeff Tuttle went to the Wichita Eagle in 1989 after working at the Herald in Jasper, Ind. He is a native of Augusta, Kan., and graduated from Kansas State University in 1987 with a journalism degree.

Photo: Page 5.

Thomas Van Dyke

San Jose Mercury News photographer Thomas Van Dyke, who was born in Canada, is a self-described air force brat: His father was in the U.S. Air Force, his mother in the Canadian. He attended San Jose State University and also worked at newspapers in Vallejo, Calif., and Reno, Nev.

Photo: Page 142.

Herb Welch

Herb Welch was born in Biloxi, Miss., and has been a photographer at the Sun Herald for 11 years. He graduated with a bachelor's degree in journalism from the University of Southern Mississippi in 1976, and has worked at the Delta Democrat-Times in Greenville and Mississippi Press Register in Pascagoula. He has won several state and regional photography awards.

Photo: Pages 44-45.

Hal Wells

University of Missouri graduate Hal Wells has been working at the Long Beach Press-Telegram for two years. He has worked at the Orange County Register and teaches part-time at California State University, Long Beach.

Photo: Pages 36-37.

Susan Winters

Susan Winters, a 10-year Philadelphia Daily News staff photographer, has won the New Jersey Photographer of the Year award and National Headliners and National Press Photographers Association awards. She studied art at Tulane University and the Cleveland Institute of Art.

Photo: Pages 74-75.

STAFF

Randy Miller   Editor

Gary Blonston   Writer

Mike Smith   Picture Editor

John Goecke   Production Editor

Andrew Countryman Copy Editor

Dave Robinson   Distribution

Perry Baker   Picture Editors
Charlie Borst
Tom Gralish
Chris Magerl
Marcia Prouse
Susan Kirkman

Marty Westman   Artist

Alexander Cruden Copy Editor

Herman Allen   Lab Technicians
Diane Bond
Helen McQuerry
Jessica Trevino

Larry Ross   Computer Output

Rose Ann McKean Adminstrative Assistants
Deborah Caverzan Scola

Knight-Ridder, Inc.
One Herald Plaza, Miami, Fla. 33132

James K. Batten
Chairman of the Board
Chief Executive Officer

P. Anthony Ridder **C.W. Baker**
President & *Group Vice President/News*
President/Newspaper Division

Richard G. Capen, Jr. **Jennie Buckner**
Vice Chairman of the Board *Vice President/News*

More than 24,000 marines parading at Camp Lejeune, N.C., stand at attention before shipping out to the Mideast.
JEFF SINER
Charlotte Observer

This book was produced and designed on a Macintosh II CX computer. Type was set in Bodoni 2 Book and ITC Franklin Gothic Demi from Adobe Systems; page composition was done with Aldus Pagemaker and Freehand software; camera-ready masters were produced on an Ultre 94 Imagesetter.

Photographic images recorded on color negative and transparency films from Kodak and Fuji were printed on Kodak Professional Ektacolor Ultra paper.

Printed by Gaylord Printing, Detroit, Mich.